Living in the Question

An Exploration of Formlessness, Change, and Healing

Michael Maley, Ph.D.

Bodysmart Publications
Minneapolis

Published by the author. Address inquiries to:
> Bodysmart Publications
> P.O. Box 1184
> Minnetonka, MN 55345-0184

Cover layout, chapter illustrations, and figure graphics by Stephen Bolles.

Cataloging in Publication Data:

Maley, Michael J. 1938-

> Living in the Question: An Exploration of
> Formlessness, Change, & Healing.

> Includes bibliographical references and index.
> ISBN 0-9649741-0-X: $13.95
> 1. Change (Psychology). 2. Spiritual Life.
> 3. Adjustment (Psychology). 4. Life Change Events.
> 5. Spiritual Health.

I. Title

BF 637. L53M294 1995
155.2

PRINTED IN THE UNITED STATES OF AMERICA

*To Tricia, love of my life
and dearest friend*

Acknowledgements

It pleasures me to acknowledge how much help and support I have been given in the project. I graciously thank Tricia, my wife, whose constant support and encouragement made it possible to do something this time consuming; Donna Taylor, a friend and teacher in matters dealing with spiritual change; Stephen Bolles, who did a substantial amount of work helping with formatting, giving me editorial assistance, designing the cover layout, and creating the figures and illustrations; Holly Einess, the editor of the self-published version; Robert Hilton, for his helpful comments and sage look at the contents; Miriam Pew, Ben Shapiro, and Michael Smith, who, as friendly readers, made the material more readable and understandable; and my friends, clients and students whose stories fill these pages. Like many projects, this was a group effort and I deeply thank those who helped me put my thoughts into words.

For permission to reprint excerpts, the author is grateful to the following:
Ariel Press, Publishers for *Practical Mysticism*, Underhill, Evelyn, 1942; Center Press, for *Somatic Reality*, Keleman, Stanley, 1979; Element Books, for *The Chasm of Fire*, Tweedie, Irina, 1979; Paulist Press, for *John of the Cross: Selected Writings*, Kavanaugh, Kieran, 1979; Random House, Inc. for *Resilience*, Flach, Frederic, 1988; and W.W. Norton Company, Inc, for *Letters To A Young Poet*, Rilke, Maria Rainer, 1934.

Contents

I want to beg you, as much as I can,
dear sir, to be patient toward all that is
unsolved in your heart and try to
love the questions themselves
like locked rooms and like
books that are written
in a very foreign
tongue.

Do not now seek the answers, which
cannot be given you because you
would not be able to live them.
And the point is, to live
everything.

Live the questions now. Perhaps you will
then gradually, without noticing it, live
along some distant day into the
answer.

R.M. Rilke
reprinted by permission

The Territory

I wrote this essay for and about students of the process of personal change—those individuals who have dedicated at least some part of their life task to consciously developing themselves personally and spiritually. Anyone who has taken up the struggle to become a more conscious human being knows well that to achieve progress toward a goal such as this requires a number of skills, not the least of which is some understanding of how change takes place and some of the stages that we go through in changing the nature of the self experience. **Change itself**[1] becomes an important focus as well as whatever specific thing we wish to change. Since this was my journey as well, I wrote these chapters to deepen my own understanding of the process and so I could teach it to my students and those therapists and healers who support others going through the experience.

The material in this essay is my attempt to elaborate on what I have felt are some of the most important aspects of the experience of personal change and psychospiritual development. One of these is a class of experiences that I am calling **formlessness**—an energy that enters the transformation process in the stage when old behaviors, attitudes, feelings, and belief systems that have previously defined the self have dissolved. When this happens, people find themselves in the state of "not clear what to do next"; "not sure who I am"; "without purpose"; "lost and empty"; or unable to experience much of a connection to their familiar personal self—a time when everything seems to be **in the Question.** Experiences of formlessness accompany a wide variety of situations in which people attempt to cope with new situations or become involved in the process of personal transformation, since all change requires the dissolution of an old way of being as new ways of thinking, feeling, and behaving are being constructed. Formlessness can be a temporary state or a much more prolonged condition, depending on the depth of the changes that are in process.

As the basic experience of formlessness becomes more familiar, it develops into an attitude or frame of mind called **Living in the Question. This attitude is a more or less permanent state of consciousness—one of the tools of self-discovery—in which the experience of changing (or becoming) is felt to be more important than being something in particular.** We experience our self more as a creative process than as something fixed in form (like a particular role or an isolated island of experience). The self experience is something that changes all the time, growing, deepening and developing with a delicate balance between purpose, choice, and spontaneity. Living in the Question is a fluid way of being in the world—a way of existing that embraces the idea that we change through connection. It holds an attitude that values asking questions and receiving answers, but uses each answer as a platform for the next question. Adopting and working with this attitude becomes a very powerful tool in the journey of self-realization. Living in the Question is a way of talking about the end product of a series of personal transformations in which the individual touches formlessness and integrates this experience into his or her psyche.

Also discussed in this essay is a model of the change

process called the **Formula for Change,** and a description of the phases through which formlessness enters the transformation process and change happens. It has been my experience that personal emotional healing, the development of the self into multidimensionality, and the fostering of spiritual experience are part of a continuous process and not entirely separate activities. They all share the task of challenging fixed self structures and entering the change process. Although the goals might be different the process is similar.

In this essay, I have used the term *psychospiritual development* to refer to a wide range of activities and learning experiences whose purpose is to bring more consciousness to the experience of self. This learning process will often involve some therapeutic work to heal emotional wounds; participation in spiritual practices to develop personal control and discipline; exploration of energetic disciplines involving alternative states of awareness; and a quest for spiritual knowledge. At the heart of this process, however, **the experience of selfhood** is constantly changing. The primary goal of this journey is to both discover and create a consciousness of self larger than the one you have at present. By larger I mean an experience of self that begins to include more of the dimensions that can come with being a soul incarnated and alive in a body—a vital physical experience; an emotional life with depth and passion; consciousness brought to all aspects of the psyche (both healthy and unhealthy); a mental life that seeks an understanding of what it is to be human; and a spiritual life in which touching planes of existence both inside and outside the self is possible. Although this essay focuses on the psychological experience of allowing formlessness to enter the change process, the principles appear to be applicable to many levels of spiritual experience and development.

The third focus of this essay is another process that seems to be an important element in healing and trans-

formation. In this process, known as **blending**, healthy
parts of the self are mobilized to reach inward to touch
the unhealthy isolated sides. For blending to occur, personal consciousness and choice are mobilized, as are the
abilities to explore and connect to previously hidden
parts of the self. By extension, the healing of self also
involves a blending process with others. **Both personal
healing and personal development involve making
connections to others that facilitate their growth as well
as our own.** This approach means that psychospiritual
development and personal change require movement
and flexibility in the bodymind, connections to the world
external to the self, and a greater witness or observer
consciousness to choices being made. It means being able
to **move, change, connect, and choose.** It is, essentially,
identical with the process of **problem solving**. This particular way of looking at spiritual development was first
taught to me by a mentor known as the Teacher[2].

The contents of this book are as follows: Chapters 1
and 2 are a discussion of the ways in which the energy
of formlessness enters the transformation process and a
review of some of the many faces of formlessness. Chapter 3 provides a summary of the Formula for Change—
an important tool summarizing the stages of the change
process. Chapters 4 and 5 contain more detailed descriptions of certain phases of the change experience surrounding the experience of letting go of old ways of being. Chapter 6 discusses the experiences of voids and
chaos, and, along with Chapter 7, elaborates on the idea
of how to "walk through formlessness" and begin to
move with questions. Chapter 8 is a discussion of the
process of blending, and Chapter 9 is a summary of the
idea of Living in the Question.

My hope is that the material will be as alive and as
useful to you as it was to me, both in my own growth
and in my work with others.

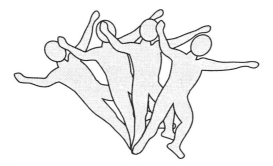

Chapter 1

Change and the Experience of Space

Change always involves an encounter with psychophysical structures—either the formation or dissolution of fixed networks of thoughts, feelings, and response patterns.

In the preface, I made a brief reference to one definition of formlessness as "being in the question." What does this mean?

I think I could characterize much of my early life as being much more interested in answers than in questions. I wanted certainty, security, stability, predictability, control. It was difficult not to know what might happen and even more difficult to let go of control once things began to happen. Like many others, my way of coping was to seek answers for what was unknown and frightening. What will I be when I grow up? How do you get rid of this problem? When will I be finished? How much longer will I have to wait? Do you love me? Will I have enough money? Why don't you do it *this* way? I am a teacher, a Caucasian, a Christian, a Democrat. An answer puts a form and a structure on situations. It helps us know what has happened and what to look forward to in the future. Answers represent explanations, something fixed and known—something to build on and be sure of—a foundation, a limit, a container, a blanket, a wall. You can *do something* with an answer—build on it, organize around it, defend against it, or rest easy.

The quest for answers seems to be the search for truth as well. In science and medicine, the goal of an answer is to approximate the truth. Answers are models for reality and help us organize the world into something understandable and real. Yet as we know, these models change. Newtonian physics became quantum physics, and allopathic medicine is becoming more holistic, including the spiritual and energetic dimensions of the person. Answers change as knowledge increases or reality shifts and **what is true is only true for a time. After that, it is a lie.**[1]

A question, on the other hand, has no such fixed form. It is only the beginning of a form, the next step after nothing. Questions are ways in which we begin to extend toward something. They are possibilities and anticipations. By their nature, they are also risks. You give up control when you ask a true question, since you have no way of knowing what will come back as the answer. Questions are a way of entering the mystery of something—a way of allowing it to show you what it is.

Like the Buddhist concept of the beginner's mind, a question is an attitude toward knowledge and the truth. To be in the question is to be open to receive whatever might emerge. It is not for those who hate surprises.

This essay is about the experience of change and about the role that "being in the question" plays in the change process. What we seek to change in psychospiritual work is the structure of our individual self and our ability to connect to the world. If our connections are limited or fixed and unchanging, so is our self structure. **The fixed parts of ourselves—the unchanging belief systems, emotional expressions, sensation patterns, or relationship rituals are like answers.** Our identity is *an answer.* The difficulty is that sometimes those answers that we have (and are) are very old and we constructed them in other times in different circumstances. Insofar as our current reality is different, these answers become lies, and no longer function in our best interest. They are no longer alive. So how do we change these old answers and lies into questions, and how does the structure of the self become more of a question and more open to change? These questions and others are the primary subject of this work.

Change, Structure, and Selfhood

From a psychospiritual perspective, **change always involves an encounter with structure**[2], either the physical structures of the body, emotional patterns, belief systems, or the surrounding energetic structures of the human form. Change means an increase or a decrease in the number or the rigidity of the behaviors that connect us to the world and make up the forms that constitute our individuality. Life demands many such changes. Emerging through early development and forming a personality; learning about the world throughout childhood and adolescence; staying connected to our children and friends as they change over the years; maintaining a vibrant marriage over time; touching parts of the self never before encountered; creating new forms for self-expression—all require significant changes in the structures and behaviors we use for such connections. I have to surrender those parts of myself that would like to have it only my way or would like to control, possess, or own someone, and replace them with behaviors and beliefs that allow change in myself and allow acceptance of a much wider range of energies in others. All of these adjustments are necessary for a mature life. The structure of the self has to constantly shift and change in order to stay related to the world in healthy ways.

The early development of the child is the story of how self structures form in response to connections to the world to ensure further survival, growth, and the formation of a personality. As far as we know, the early psychological world of the newborn infant is filled with the experience of formlessness—substance, yet not much form. No real sense of itself as a separate individual has been established, and there are no fixed perceptions of the world as this or that, good or bad. The self of the infant is not the individual infant, but the mother-infant unit. The caregiver is the auxiliary self, part of the early ego structure of the child that provides many of the capacities that the young infant has not yet developed. Only the most basic structures relevant for physical survival appear to be operating. These structures are tentative and very fluid in their attachment to the external world.

One of the inherent capacities of the human nervous system is the ability to build structure—that is, to build **couplings** with the external world that enable the developing infant and child to maintain the connections that enhance its own life processes. Couplings are organized responses to particular inputs that enable the child to make and maintain a connection to mother, father, and the rest of the world. These couplings are the evidence that psychological structures are beginning to form—the ones that reflect learnings that have occurred and show recognition of familiar experiences. The developing child's consciousness reflects couplings with his or her inside world (how the child feels internally and how the body responds), with developing emotions, and with caregivers. Associative networks develop as these three sources of information get linked. The growing child begins to respond in and to the world in these packages— body, feeling, and object. In the beginning of development, these packages of couplings are based on survival contacts. The child has couplings for food, for touch, for love, for internal body states; for external objects; for good experiences, for bad experiences. Initially they emerge separately and discretely, and only after two or three years of development do these patterns overlap and join together to form larger associative networks. They begin to organize into patterns of behavior that look like a cohesive self,[3] that is, they are consistent responses to connections to the outside world. These behavioral forms are the first answers of the child to questions of contact and survival. They are mostly fluid, as parents notice how quickly their child adapts to changes in the external world in order to maintain connection. Both parents and children change in these interactions, each trying to find the other and reinforce the growing bond. Trauma makes these couplings rigid, whereas love and support allow them to move and change with development.

So the psychological world of children is filled with experiences of **formlessness and questions** while in the process of finding answers. Mental structures, like their ideas and identities, are fluid. Everything is experimental, including who they are and what they believe and trust. They are "open" to experience. Whatever they touch impacts them. The world is taken in and forms the self and the self extends into the world. Questions abound and answers are held only as long as they prove useful. A sense of spaciousness and motion pervades the psychic life of the healthy child and the experience of self constantly changes if a nurturing environment supports such fluidity. "Goodenough" mothering, the ability to see the world as safe, sufficient stimulation, and loving contacts are some of the factors that support these structures and help the child make connections to the world that hold spaciousness and formlessness. Moving the body, being curious, asking questions, using one's imagination, dreaming, experiencing the etheric world— all contain the fluidity of creative expression and allow more space, more room for freedom of expression. Interpersonal relationships can also have this sense of space. Emotions like trust, the anticipation of pleasure, hopefulness, optimism, and love all contain the spaciousness necessary for the later development of even more creative states. In young children it is not unusual to see their "essence" showing through—those fundamental energies that will be with them throughout life if they do not close down through trauma.

The sense of space present in the young child's psychological structure maintains itself throughout development in the flexibility of his or her movements and the fluidity of thinking and problem solving. The child continues to challenge ideas and concepts, question authority, and try on and abandon identities as more and more couplings with the world are practiced and discarded. Moving through development means replacing the structures of one stage with the possibilities of the next. With support, the person is able to reach toward the world and let new connections emerge. Psychological health and maturity grow at each stage of the life cycle when there are supports for making connections to one's body, emotional systems, mental functions, and spiritual formulations. If that can happen, the structures of the self are able to hold space and formlessness. Creativity is retained. Spiritual experience will be sought after as a natural experience, not rejected as irrelevant to life, since its essential qualities—fluidity and formlessness—have been present since childhood and can be embraced.

In the developing person, there are many levels and systems of connection that reflect passages into adulthood. Connections to mother or the primary caregivers are first and help form the infant's connection to his or her body and mental capacities. Then, the child's world expands to family and peers. Partnership connections are next, as are connections to community, nation, world, and the larger universe. These couplings are the medium by which the self emerges, becomes more and more complex, and can develop depth, breadth, and multidimensionality. Healthy foundations in body, mind, and emotions early in life form the basis for further growth as development proceeds. Trauma, lack of early support, and rigidity in any one of these coupling networks limit the ability to connect and stop psychospiritual growth until those limits are consciously identified. Too often, in the passage to adulthood, the child loses those self structures that embrace openness—an eagerness to learn, connect to others, and hold questions. Somewhere along the way, the self becomes too structuralized, too rigid in its forms. The investment in staying the same wins out over the messages of change. Spiritual development stops since the structures of the self cannot embrace the formless experiences of the change process and the subtle energies of spiritual life. Essence loses to the demands of the physical world and the inertia of solidity.

Structural Change and Healing

For many individuals, entering into the healing process is the first way in which they become conscious of rigid forms in their body, emotions, or behavior. Working with fixed self structures is the basis of a wide variety of psychological and physical interventions associated with bodymind healing. Examples of this might include:

•ridding the body of scar tissue after injury or childhood accidents to restore range of motion and more circulation to damaged tissue;
•loosening the chronic muscular holding patterns of emotional attitudes to release the feelings associated with past trauma or to extend one's emotional range;
•letting go of fixed patterns of addiction or compulsive actions;
•changing negative or fixed belief systems formed in early life that interfere with intimacy or the forming of new relationships;
•challenging assumptions about the self that limit

achievement, performance, or abundance;
   • examining the blocking beliefs or perceptual habits that interfere with connections to the spiritual world.

These encounters with fixed ways of being (especially if they create isolation and limit connection) constitute the core of therapy and personal growth work. What makes change difficult is that these structures are persistent, immovable, and chronically drain energy from other functions that might promote more life and pleasure. They constrict instead of expand possibilities of being—they support contraction of experience instead of spaciousness. Curiously, most individuals never challenge these "ego structures" unless pain levels are high. Once established, many of these structures are never even noticed, unless challenged by a person getting close to you (like a partner, a mentor, or a teacher) or unless you have some kind of breakthrough experience that reveals another way of being. Answers seem to perpetuate themselves into the inertia of unconsciousness. Far too many people remain "asleep" to their own possibilities because of the dominance in the psyche of these fixed structures that determine experience.

The Polyphrenic Self

There is a long and fascinating history of discussions between students of spiritual development and psychological theorists regarding the nature of the "self". As these explorations have evolved over time, neither schools of spiritual development, cognitive science, nor depth psychology have been able to locate or demonstrate the existence of a unitary self structure that exists in the individual's inner space and simply awaits discovery (see Varela, Thompson & Rosch, 1992). There is nothing like a "self" if, by that, one means a "me"—a single structural form separate and unique and holding constant. Those structures that people think of as their "personal selves"—the ego identifications and defenses that make up much of the content of the mind—continue to shift and change so much as personal exploration deepens that there is no single unitary structure that ends up being anything like a fixed individual self.

Psychospiritual development is a process in which rigid self-identifications and defenses are dissolved to allow the discovery and development of a healthier self. As they do, at least two important experiences begin to emerge. The self structure becomes both more multiple and more formless—that is, less structured and less easily identified as a single entity. The development of the self celebrates experiences of being polyphrenic, many faceted, and multidimensional. As consciousness expands, both healthy and unhealthy patterns are revealed. Not only the wounded child emerges and is embraced, but the creative child, plus the lover, the artist, the healer, the warrior, the mystic, gods and goddesses within. Each of these selves or self structures holds the potential for contacting different aspects of the multidimensional reality that composes the spiritual life. Our personal and spiritual selves are holograms of psychospiritual reality, and there are as many potential selves within as there are realities to connect to externally. The many different self structures that make up ours internal world foster more possible connection to the external world. These connections, in turn, produce more impact on the self, and more change. The journey of psychospiritual development emphasizes going inward to find that multi-dimensionality, and then moving outward to create more connection to the world. This connection further develops the energies discovered in the inward search.

The Formless Self

When an individual is able to embrace experiences of formlessness, no matter how temporary, a shift occurs in the feelings that form the basis of one's sense of uniqueness and individuality. What is thought of as the self begins to change. The person shifts his or her identification from individual ego states (specific answers that stay constant) to more energetic and far more formless experiences of the bodymind. That is, as I deepen my self experience, I continue to shift the referents for my individuality from the specific roles I might play or the defenses I utilize (e.g., I am a psychologist, a teacher, a "nice guy" or a "bad boy"), or a particular experience of my body (e.g., I am tight in my shoulders, ungrounded and spacey), to a more internal process of knowing about my uniqueness (e.g., I am sensing my individual energy pattern separate from you or my body separate from my consciousness), to knowing about myself by how I am embedded in a larger reality (e.g., I know myself through my connections to the world or I am part of something much larger than myself). There are different ways to experience the self with each passing phase of spiritual work. These knowings about the self are passages and expansions of consciousness. In these transitions, the process of knowing who we are becomes far more formless in its nature and the search for self becomes not a search for a single object or an answer, but an engagement in a complex process of experiencing and connecting. The movements between personal individuality and blending with a larger spiritual reality become more fluid and can coexist in ways that become more and more difficult to describe. As spiritual process deepens further, states are experienced in which all vestiges of the "I" are lost in the connection to the spiritual universe. The self experience includes within its grasp space and formlessness alternating with form and connection to the physical world.

As an individual matures and develops, his or her personal self is created more than it is discovered. We literally make ourselves. Choice becomes paramount. The commitment to the process of spiritual development requires that the personal self—those psychophysical structures that mediate our connection to the physical world—has to expand further to become a channel for deeper experiences of life. These channels include connections to more and more formless worlds—psychic life, etheric beings, spiritual energies, and personal essences. These worlds of experience are far more fluid realities than the solid physical world, and substantial changes in the self are required in order to maintain the connections. The self itself becomes less defined by specific structures that promote only individuality and becomes instead a network for acts of connection. **These acts of connection are the self structure. The self is formed by its connections.** To maintain connections to spiritual reality external to us requires increased fluidity and movement within the self. A similar process occurs as we attempt to develop connections to more subtle energetic movements within the body. The deeper energies of the self—those essential states of value, compassion, courage, wisdom, and presence—require that we move our isolation and defenses aside and allow more connection and expression out into the world. As these energies move through the bodymind, they have the effect of changing our structure even more and altering the form of our personal selves.

To engage this process, the personal self must become more fluid and multidimensional and learn how to hold the experience of formlessness more and more. The individual who can have a body that lives with the earth and touch a higher self that lives in spiritual reality is a fluid self indeed, and for someone to attain that level of connection involves a process of continual stretching into new ways of being. It means learning to

live in the question, since it is **change itself** that characterizes the system and **learning how to change** is an important part of deepening self-understanding.

The ability to couple with the world and connect in
ways that are fluid and changing is the essence of both
personal change and spiritual development. The next
chapter illustrates the many faces of formlessness and
how this experience works to open the self to the possibility of psychospiritual growth.

Chapter 2

Formlessness

*Formlessness is associated with
the process of transformation.*

The energy of formlessness is a universal experience. Every person has had some contact with it, some time when she or he has touched one of its many aspects. Whenever we try to consciously change something about ourselves, whether it be an attitude, a belief, a way of looking at things, or a way of acting, there is always something that gets destroyed while something new is being created. Each time we become something different, we have to let go of something we were, and there is always a moment, a space, or a gap of time that lies between what we have given up and what we are about to create. That space and time crucible between what we were and what we will become is what I am calling the experience of **formlessness or "being in the question."** It is within the boundaries of this experience that much is learned about the experience of personal and psychospiritual change and about the nature of the self. The goal of this chapter is to present the different ways in which the experience of formlessness occurs in our lives and to look at what can be learned from those experiences.

Experiences of Formlessness

There are a number of ways that the experience of being temporarily "formless" can touch an individual's life. Paradoxically, the experience of being formless itself has many forms. Figure 1 illustrates some of the ways formlessness comes into an individual's life. The text that follows describes them in more detail.

In any one person, formlessness can manifest itself as a result of a shift in ones external circumstances, as a part of a physical or mental illness, as an internal shift in ones identity, or as a religious experience. Being without structure—either in one's external circumstances or as an experience of the self—can be a transitional and fluid state or can become stagnant and seem to last forever.

As a way of looking at the many ways in which this experience can occur, here are some of the faces of formlessness:

•Formlessness is present when you lose a person, a role, or a commitment that has been an important part of your life. It is present with the distress that occurs when the meaning or direction of your life changes as a result of something that happens to you.

•Formlessness is present when you are no longer able to do what was familiar or usual because your circumstances have changed. It is present with the fear of the unfamiliar.

•Formlessness is present when you have been in control and suddenly you find yourself not in control and in the midst of chaos. It means not having an answer where you had one before—the loss of certainty, predictability, and what used to work for you.

•Formlessness can occur when you make a developmental transition. . . when new needs, desires, or values arise and you have not yet formed a way to express

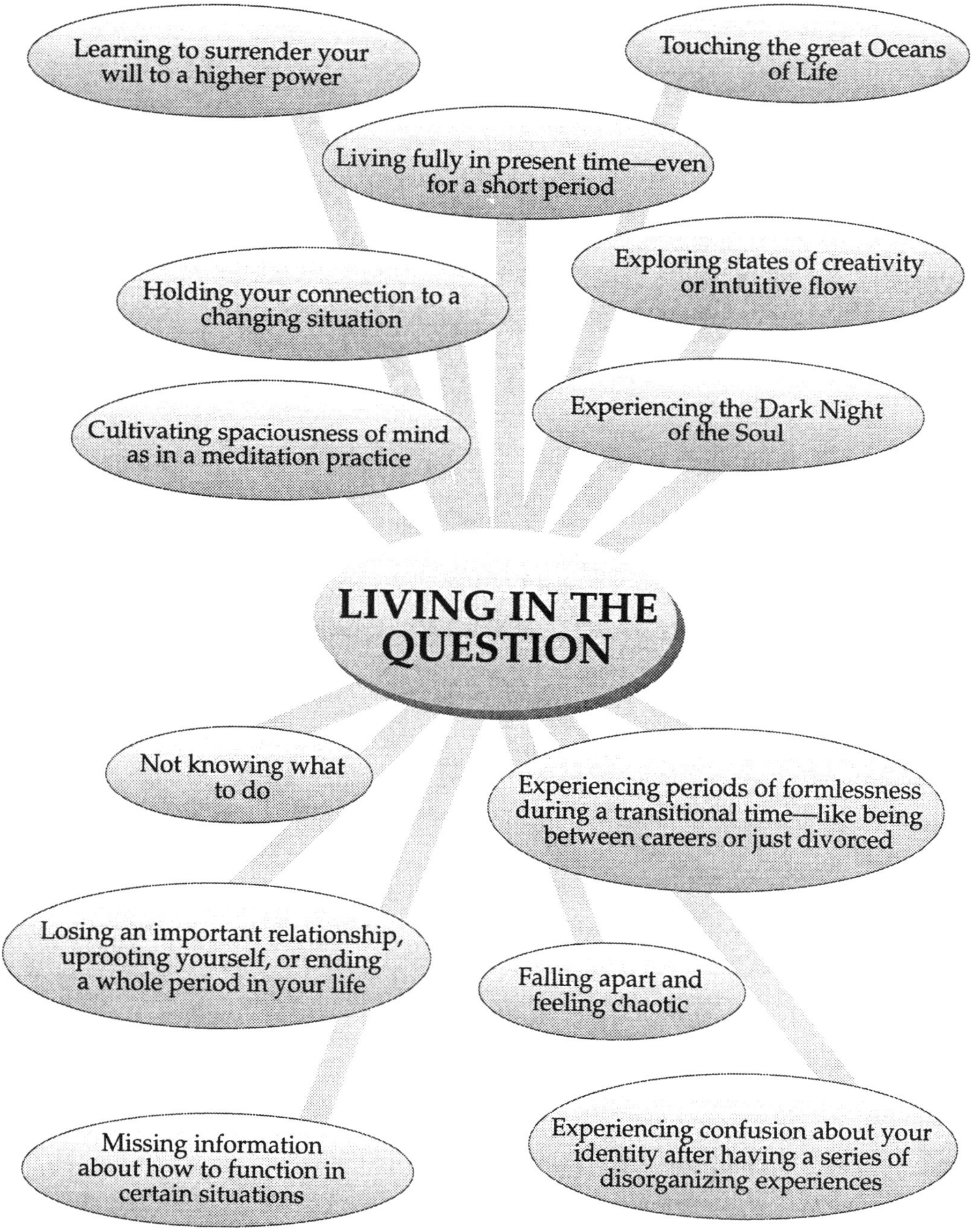

Learning to surrender your will to a higher power

Touching the great Oceans of Life

Living fully in present time—even for a short period

Exploring states of creativity or intuitive flow

Holding your connection to a changing situation

Cultivating spaciousness of mind as in a meditation practice

Experiencing the Dark Night of the Soul

LIVING IN THE QUESTION

Not knowing what to do

Experiencing periods of formlessness during a transitional time—like being between careers or just divorced

Losing an important relationship, uprooting yourself, or ending a whole period in your life

Falling apart and feeling chaotic

Missing information about how to function in certain situations

Experiencing confusion about your identity after having a series of disorganizing experiences

Figure 1. Living in the Question:
Some Examples of Formlessness

the new feelings.

•Formlessness touches you when something happens that changes your idea of who you are. . . when you are questioning your beliefs and motivations. . . when something inside you has shifted and the old ways no longer make sense.

•Formlessness is present when you have been something all your life that your family or someone else dictated and now you are making your own decisions and choices. . . when you say "I want to be who I am" but you don't know who this is yet.

•Formlessness is present when you move from a negative self-image to a positive one. . . when you begin claiming who you are and find that there are many parts of yourself still undeveloped. . . when you move out of identifying yourself in terms of your ego defenses and begin to reach deeper for your real self.

•Formlessness is touching you when you find that you do not know how to do something. . . when you contact places of unknowing and are reaching for both questions and answers.

•Formlessness comes forth when you begin the process of disidentification (altering the self experience) on a conscious level and reach for spiritual experience. . . when you begin your own spiritual awakening and the opening to the mystery.

•Formlessness is present with the anguish of contacting areas of deep emptiness and void within the self. . . when you touch the Dark Night of your Soul and lose your connection to God.

•Formlessness is with you when you touch the mystery of life. . . when you ask questions that have many answers and you move joyfully into the feminine, the vastness, the Oceans, and the great Void.

•**Formlessness is the essence of the Creative Process, Spirit, and Soul.**

Several things become apparent in reading this list.

First, as mentioned earlier, the experience itself has a number of faces. Formlessness manifests itself in many forms and is present in many common experiences that lead to or provide the opportunity for profound personal change. **Formlessness accompanies the process of transformation.**

Second, formlessness can be present in both deeply disturbing and extraordinarily joyful moments. It can be present when people touch their deepest emptiness and also present as a core of certain sacred experiences. It can produce a sense of awe and wonder as well as anguish or terror. This suggests that, by itself, **formlessness does not have any particular affective tone. That is, it is not an emotion or associated with any particular emotion.**

Third, it is not unusual for an individual to have experienced many of the levels summarized in the list— sometimes together, sometimes at different times. So formlessness is not associated with any one kind of experience, but it can be present and working in many different situations. What this suggests is that formlessness is more like an energy band—a type of vibratory state or chaotic phenomenon that occurs when forms like belief systems, attitudes, or movement patterns are being changed. When this energy touches form, it can alter that form. That is, **formlessness is present when forms break down or it can help break down forms and facilitate change. It can operate at any level of the bodymind—that is, a person can let go of and change thinking patterns, emotional responses, body structure, or behaviors. Formlessness can happen to a person; it can be cultivated to initiate change; or like any other experience, it can be avoided, fled from, judged, or loved.**

Fourth, **formlessness is very alive as an energy.** Like the winds of change, it pulsates with life. It is not dead, passive, resigned, or stuck. Since it accompanies the movement and dissolution of structure, its intrinsic spontaneity and fluidity contains energy and creative potential. If the individual is not afraid of the experience, those moments or periods between answers can be full of energy and feeling. Also, formlessness is not necessarily associated with dissociation or disconnection. Although these movements can both reveal and produce eventual formlessness, the experience itself is too alive in the present to be identical with defenses that remove an individual from living in the moment. **Formlessness is a living experience of forms changing, not one of controlling experience.**

As a way of looking at these kinds of experiences and processes in more detail, it would help to consider some of the most common ways in which formlessness can enter a person's life—by a change in external circumstances; by internal shifts in the sense of self; or by the pursuit of spiritual experience.

The Loss of Familiar External Structures

•Formlessness is present when you lose a person, a role, or a commitment that has been an important part of your life. It is present with the distress that occurs when the "meaning" or direction of your life changes as a result of something that happens to you.

•Formlessness is present when you are no longer able to do what was familiar or usual because your circumstances have changed. It is present with the fear of the unfamiliar.

•Formlessness is present when you have been in control and suddenly you find yourself not in control and in the midst of chaos. It means not having an "answer" where you had one before—the loss of certainty, predictability, and what used to work for you.

The experience of formlessness comes sharply into

focus when there is a large or an abrupt change in one's external environment and one cannot respond in usual ways. What was familiar falls apart or changes and one's life has to take a new direction. Everyone encounters these transitional times at one point in their life. Losing one's job or retiring, moving and changing neighborhoods, becoming separated or divorced, having children grow up and leave home, losing a spouse or a close friend, having an accident or becoming ill and adjusting to new limitations, taking time off after a long period of being very busy, or taking on a new job and not being given formal work assignments, all produce a change in the external structure that guided and directed behavior and often gave meaning and purpose to one's life. When these personal anchors get pulled away, the result can be deeply disturbing. The change in structure can leave the person "formless" in the sense of *having no familiar way to act or be* and being challenged to come up with a whole new set of behaviors, attitudes, and purposes for life. If the experience was not chosen or predicted, and there has not been a time of preparation, the ensuing formlessness can be a very difficult experience. A client described the experience like this:

> The death of my husband was devastating to me. Every aspect of my life revolved around him—from the time we spent at breakfast to our overlapping schedules around work to our vacations. I feel as if I'm living in a void without his presence.

These kinds of losses or changes demonstrate how much meaning people place in the roles they play and in what they do—how attached the sense of self is to the external world. The loss of these familiar patterns of behavior and attachment can have an enormous effect on how stable, how important, how needed, how loved, and how connected to the world the person feels.

This aspect of the formlessness experience—the one

created by transitions in life—has been described by many authors. *Chaos* (Flach, 1988), the *middle ground* (Keleman, 1979), and the *neutral zone* (Bridges, 1980) are a few of the terms used to elaborate the nature of this experience. Many of these descriptions have emphasized the importance of this experience as a temporary, but necessary, part of the change process. In these models formlessness is an experience that comes **between** stages, a creative void in which old forms have dissolved and there is both the opportunity and the need to make a new behavior, to experience new feelings, or to receive new understandings.

In Stanley Keleman's book *Somatic Reality,* the **middle ground** is a stage that occurs between endings and beginnings. He refers to the middle ground as "the womb of the unbounded self" and gives these exquisite descriptions of the process:

> Middle ground follows an ending. There is a pause, a swelling, a tremendous flood of mixed emotions, sensations and dreams of the future. It is a transitional phase, a no-man's-land, the cauldron of our biological process out of which we can form a new connection.

> It is what happens at the end of harvest before the new shoots come up—the same deep processes are occurring that happen between inhalation and exhalation, between blossoming and re-blossoming.

> The middle ground is a receptive and conceiving state; it is both the birth of form and the formless; it is a place where things are begotten and conception itself touches us.

William Bridges, in his book *Transitions,* names the **neutral zone** as a time of reorganization and reformation of attitudes, goals, and self-identity. Frederic Flach, in his book *Resilience,* refers to a period of **chaos** in which:

> I began to see falling apart as a normal—in fact, necessary—response to significant changes within ourselves or in our

environment... this is when we become severely destabilized. Our internal or external structure may disintegrate into chaos, and the eventual outcome of such chaos is totally unpredictable.

All of these writers are elaborating on one of the basic features of the formlessness experience—namely that something has come apart and there is a period of relative chaos and disorganization that ensues and precedes the formation of a new way of being. This perspective implies that the energetic experience of formlessness—because it sits at the very core of the change process—is an experience that needs to be understood and integrated, rather than feared or ignored. The view that the destructuring and formlessness experience is an **essential** one for change to take place is important because it leads to further discussions about how such an experience can be accepted and worked with, rather than avoided. The process of "walking through formlessness" becomes an important part of the reintegration experience.

When people experience the formlessness created by the loss of important persons or roles in their life, there is almost always a **parallel process** of loss/grief, fear/paralysis, or anger/acting out. What I mean by a parallel process is that there are two things happening at once. One is emotional (the reaction to the loss and/or the changes), and the other is the experience of not knowing how to respond to the changing conditions. One is the response to the letting go and disintegration of familiar structures and the other is about how to work with the formation of new behaviors and beliefs. The energy of formlessness is different from the emotions that might surround or accompany it. One is not more important than the other; they are just different experiences and both need recognition and time for processing.

The emotional reactions that accompany transitions require processing and support to come to completion.

They always surface in times of transition and need to become conscious and be allowed to come to expression. Emotional reactions provide the individual with an immense amount of information about his or her belief systems and attitudes that would ordinarily not have become so conscious. They give one an opportunity to look more deeply into the structures of the self.

The ability to tolerate, name, and work with the emotions will often determine how the subsequent period of formlessness is approached. An individual's inability to find support to express the feelings around the transitional experience can hamper any potential for change. The mobilization of defenses can stop the work of taking stock of where you are, asking where to go next, and trying to make the next phase alive and more creative. Both emotional and creative processing suffer if the person has to "pull it all together and get functioning" too fast, or if there is no opportunity to let things not be known for a time. More than a few students of change have stated that periods of unknowing represent the greatest opportunity for new, unpredictable creative processes to emerge. In these situations, formlessness is allowed to be more present if the emotional reactions to the changes are supported and processed.

When formlessness is forced upon a person by virtue of a change in circumstances, he or she must change and adapt. New conditions require that one reorganize oneself to meet the new situation. Until one can answer some of the basic questions of survival, emotional support, and stability, there is no opportunity to relish the openness and the possibilities that this state can provide. This is not the time to actively cultivate formlessness. It is, however, an opportunity to move into one of the important aspects of the process—to learn to ask more questions; to not fixate too quickly on the first answer that comes along; and to look more deeply into the self.

During transitions, the **locus of control**[1] shifts. You were formerly in control of your world and now the only thing you can control is your reaction. If something seems to have been done to you, instead of remaining in the victim position, you have the opportunity to look at how to respond. The chance to ask questions about what to do and what to create next is perhaps the only gift that formlessness can initially provide.

Following is a good example of a person having an emotional reaction to loss or change and an additional reaction to the experience of being formless:

> The transition of divorce is a good example of this multi-layered experience, especially if one of the partners was not prepared for the breakup and has to make a new life either financially or emotionally. In the initial stages there is often a process of grieving the loss of the relationship and dealing with the fear about what the future will be like. Beyond this there is a much longer process around the spaces in the lifestyle that the divorce created and the acquisition of behaviors needed to make the next phase of life successful. For example, what are this person's goals for the next time period? How assertive is this person able to be in forming new relationships? How good are his or her boundaries with people? How well can he or she reach out? How much did the role of being married define the self? The acquisition of all these new behaviors takes time and requires the person to look carefully and consciously at what he or she needs to make life successful. This is a more or less "formless" period, in which the person comes face to face with what he or she doesn't yet know how to do. The time is full of questions with not many answers. The person can end up hating the uncertainty of it, finding the new levels of personal work too hard, and moving into new relationships based on the old patterns—for example, choosing the same kind of partner and thus allowing no shift in the quality of the relationship. Here formlessness gets aborted because it cannot be tolerated.

Certainly, emotional reactions will almost always accompany the experience of formlessness at first. We live in a culture that values being organized, having answers, moving with direction, and finding our purpose. Having none of these at certain times in life can leave a person feeling disconnected from his or her culture and/ or family. We value structure, predictability, being right, and coherence in our lives and often do not do well without it. Often the person in transition experiences a certain amount of pressure from others in his or her life to bring the period of uncertainty to a close and get organized and on track again. This means that one might end up overriding the anxiety, fear, grief, anger, judgment, and confusion that can occur along with the feeling of not knowing what to do, or what will happen next. Despair, depression, and even thoughts of suicide can come to the surface when these voids occur. Identifying, supporting, and working through these feelings allows more of the process to unfold. Then, the formlessness can be more directly experienced, and more energy for change can be tapped. As the person is able to process the emotional responses to a transition, **formlessness becomes the experience of not being defined by a familiar external structure that has in the past brought comfort, safety, definition, and direction.** It means letting go of what one thought would happen and who one thought one was, and beginning the process of asking questions.

Shifts in the Sense of Self

•Formlessness can occur when you make a developmental transition. . . when new needs, desires, or values arise and you have not yet formed a way to express the new feelings.

•Formlessness touches you when something happens that changes your idea of who you are. . . when you are questioning your beliefs and motivations. . . when something inside you has shifted and the old ways no longer make sense.

•Formlessness is present when you have been something all your life that your family or someone else dictated and now you are making your own decisions and choices...when you say "I want to be who I am" but you don't know who this is yet.

•Formlessness is present when you move from a negative self-image to a positive one. . . when you begin claiming who you are and find that there are many parts of yourself still undeveloped. . . when you move out of identifying yourself in terms of your ego defenses and begin to reach deeper for your real self.

•Formlessness is touching you when you find that you do not know how to do something. . . when you contact places of unknowing and are reaching for both questions and answers.

Developmental Transitions

Some of the most intense experiences of formlessness accompany transformations of the self-image. These shifts in a person's identity can occur with or without something external changing and requiring such a process. That is, the subjective experience of who you are begins to change. The so-called "midlife crisis" is a good example of this phenomenon. Like external structures, the internal structures of the self can change, dissolve, shift, or transform. Belief systems can change; situations that formerly brought pleasure or meaning can shift and no longer be rewarding; motivations and perceptions change as consciousness expands. The individual is left with no firm identity about which to say this is me—I know who I am. Using therapeutic work to become less defended, working with a physical or mental illness, opening up to spiritual experiences, discovering abilities like psychic awareness or mediumship, or going through an intense emotional period in which one's values are changing can all contribute to shifts in self-awareness and identity. Experiences like this can disorganize a person to the point where the old self seems foreign but the new self is not well established; and the individual enters a period of relative formlessness.

One excellent example of this process occurs in individuals who have begun to work on issues of codependency and/or addiction. After the self-destructive and addictive behaviors become conscious and under control, the healing process involves the development of self-esteem and authenticity in feelings, thoughts, and actions. The goal of the individual becomes to find oneself—to learn what one needs, to develop positive and healthy relationship skills, and to strengthen identity. In other words, it is to develop a stronger healthy side. There is often a long period of formlessness that occurs when the old self-destructive patterns have changed, when the defensive layers have dissolved, and the new patterns are being built on a day-by-day basis. The person does not have much of a self to identify with at first, but virtually builds a self from scratch.

Another example is when an individual opens up psychic or mediumship abilities. Here, a whole new set of experiences and information about self and world opens up and disrupts the usual patterning of personal experience. The experience of formlessness becomes a major aspect of this transition until the new self-image can integrate the new abilities. Any spiritual emergence like this leaves the individual in the question about the sense of self.

Still another example is when an individual suffers the loss of a spouse or a child. The emergence from the grief process involves a reidentification of the self. Losing such deep and close relationships involves the loss of self and the healing requires forming new self structures.

In this transformation new thoughts and feelings emerge, new needs or abilities arise, and the person feels more deeply than before. New requirements exist for expression, but the behaviors are not yet formed. This situation is hard to tolerate and the resulting formlessness is undesirable. There is too much uncertainty. There is frustration, tension, or too much energy to handle. The old, more defended ways of being fight for dominance. Having an internal sense of the self as a fixed entity with definition feels necessary, and its loss is a frightening experience. "I don't know who I am," or, "I want to be the way I was," is what the person says. From others they hear, I want my [friend, wife, boyfriend] to be the way they were before. Shifts in self-identity require different ways of being and require that others treat one differently as well. Some family and relationship systems are slow to make these changes; some are hostile to them. In general, allowing the energy of formlessness to become part of the process of self-development is at first an uncomfortable experience.

There are enormous individual differences in how well organized and put together the experience of the "self" is in people. At one end of the continuum are the shaky and tenuous self structures of individuals who can only tolerate close emotional contact in short bursts or fragments. In the center are the more organized self structures of well-adjusted, highly functioning, but rigid people who value control and seek answers. On the other end is the sense of spaciousness and fluidity of identity that characterize (some) spiritual teachers and individuals who are able to live with formlessness but still hold a strong connection with the world. Individuals at all points in this continuum have varying strengths and weaknesses. So, each person is different in terms of how much he or she defines the self by defenses or roles, and each will have a different reaction to the loss of external structures. Similarly, each person will require a different level of support as the locus of control shifts from external determinants of behavior (how should I act) to more internal feeling states (how do I want to act). Each person will also differ as to how much tolerance he or she has for changes in belief systems and body structure over a given time period. No matter how well or poorly organized, each individual has a different investment in the structure called the "self" and for each one, negotiating one's own experience of formlessness can be both frightening and challenging.

Deficient Emptiness and Missing Information

Other aspects of formlessness that occur with shifts in the sense of self are the experiences of void or deficient emptiness. Formlessness is often first experienced in these ways. After layers of defensiveness or compensating behaviors (like shame or being a caretaker or being a victim) have surfaced and have been partially relinquished, the individual becomes conscious of how undeveloped (or immature) he or she feels. Parts of the self have been so long in hiding that those feelings, thoughts, emotions, and behaviors cannot be adequately contacted or readily expressed. The "inner child" is one such self structure, and people sometimes find him or her totally missing or in deep hiding. There might be a lack of feelings, no spontaneity, and no inner joyfulness. Similarly, if you did not have good parenting as a child, the internal experience (or structure) of being a "loved person" might be missing. In times of uncertainty or loneliness, you cannot touch that part of the self for reassurance. Also, attempts to touch these missing parts can be very painful and can produce feelings of grief or loss. The emotional pain of the experience can be a major impediment to integrating the experience of formlessness. Since wounded child structures operate out of present time, the initial experiencing of them can pull an individual back into the past and make formlessness difficult to feel. These are risky places. One needs support to reintegrate the self while one is being exposed, and the danger of being retraumatized or reabused does still exist. Allowing formlessness to emerge under these conditions is more of an emotional process than it is under other conditions. Old emotions and painful memories of trauma seem to surround the formlessness experience and it is hard to see the energy as neutral. To negotiate formlessness requires that the person learn to trust again and learn to function from the healthy parts of the self.

Another contribution to the formless state can occur when one simply does not have certain information. To not know how to do something and to be in a situation that requires a response can produce formlessness. Getting promoted to a new job, taking on new responsibilities, moving into a new developmental state, and moving into a new level of relating in a marriage are all examples of challenges that require new skills. For many people, the coping challenge is not an unwillingness to change, but rather not knowing how to behave differently. There are hundreds of individual abilities that contribute to our behavior with other people in social and intimate situations, and many of these abilities were never taught in the family of origin or in our schooling. Not knowing how to make up after a fight, or how to ask for what you need, or how to act when you are being abused, are some common examples of what people might not have learned as children and have to face and learn as adults. Many individuals find themselves having to say to a friend, I don't know how to connect to you or love you in this situation. Most people have struggled with the issue of how to deepen their relationships with those they care about. Having voids (missing information or skills) in these areas can result in an experience of formlessness in relationships that is difficult to feel or admit to and can lead to forms of defensive behavior and disconnecting rather than connecting. These will be a person's weaknesses, not strengths, and acknowledging what one does not know can be difficult, especially if there is any shame attached to the process. Facing formlessness here means having the courage to face ones' weaknesses and work with them until they become strengths.

I will more explicitly discuss the process by which formlessness enters the realm of personal identity in the next chapters, but some basic principles are apparent from the above examples: **(1) Shifts in the sense of the self can come from trying to adjust to external changes or can be due to internally generated movements. Either way, formlessness will accompany the process. (2) Some degree of formlessness is present at every level of the self—that is, everyone has voids and missing knowledge about how to connect to the world. (3) Formlessness offers the opportunity to regard the self not as a "thing" but as a creative, transformational process. Encountering formlessness as part of self-growth can lead one to this experience.**

Spiritual Awakenings

•Formlessness comes forth when you begin the process of disidentification (altering the self experience) on a conscious level and reach for spiritual experience. . . when you begin your own spiritual awakening and the opening to the mystery.

•Formlessness is present with the anguish of contacting areas of deep emptiness and void within the self. . . when you touch the Dark Night of your Soul and lose your connection to God.

•Formlessness is with you when you touch the mystery of life. . . when you ask questions that have many answers and you move joyfully into the feminine, the vastness, the Oceans, and the great Void.

•Formlessness is the essence of the Creative Process,

Spirit, and Soul.

There is one final dimension of the formlessness experience that I would like to discuss—the process of actually cultivating the experience of space, fluidity, and an openness to questions. This type of formlessness is experienced in a variety of ways, encompasses the movements of both the mind and the body, and carries within it the seeds of spiritual awakening and sacred experience.

To pursue the spiritual dimensions of the self requires that there be an opening into formlessness. Who knows what one's basic nature is? Who can predict what will happen when one says, "I wish to be more conscious," or, "I wish to know myself"? Who knows what one is like as a spiritual being? Who knows what qualities of energy one has until these energies emerge? You cannot predict the outcome of your spiritual development ahead of time, nor control the process totally once initiated. The ability to return to the question is a fundamental skill and an attitude that will yield greater immersion in the process of change and growth.

Disidentification

One of the most basic ways to invite formlessness into the growth process is through the exercise of disidentification. This procedure involves consciously dis-attaching one's identity from the various levels of the self until the observer function or "witness" becomes more developed and is experienced as separate from the process being observed (Assagioli, 1965). If I practice the basic exercise of disidentification—"I have a body, but I am not my body; I have feelings, but I am not my feelings; I have thoughts, but I am not my thoughts"— one outcome is that my witness becomes strengthened and the particular forms and contents of my mind become more and more conscious. This experience helps us to look at and accept the structures and forms that we invested energy in and said we were (our answers), and brings the very definition of the self into the question. It is a powerful exercise with many long-term effects when practiced regularly, since it begins to shift many belief systems we hold about who or what we might be. **It opens one to the possibility that the self is not something permanent, not a thing, but is a creative process of organizing and connecting.**

The exercise of disidentification also embodies some of the major principles inherent in the change process: **(1) The process of identification itself is an "answer," and change requires that it be brought into question. (2) By bringing formlessness into a process you learn that the "you" you have identified with is not in control of the developmental process taking place. In other words, formlessness is the experience through which we learn that other parts of the self, previously outside awareness, seek expression, and often control our reactions and choices.** Disidentification is one of the steps in the process of leaving behind old answers, opening to new experiences of the self, and learning to handle what emerges as one becomes more open to change.

The direct experience of space is one of the consequences of successful disidentification, especially when separating from fixed structures related to one's body-image. In his book *The Void*, A. H. Almaas describes the experiences of space that occur in therapeutic work in which the individual is able to let go of self- and body-image structures. In his view, the experience of space is a necessary stepping stone to the emergence of the Essence (as contrasted with the personality) of the human being. In his transformational process, the Diamond Approach, the experience of space is an important component of personal and spiritual development.

Many spiritual traditions, notably Buddhism, include practices that involve the "emptying" of the mind.

These practices, like Vipassana mindfulness meditation, help one develop an awareness of the mental structures that make up one's personal identity. A disclipline such as this directly cultivates more formlessness in one's mental life and consciousness. It allows one to experience the "field of mindfulness" independent of its contents and to blend consciousness with all mental operations and structures. This process has an application to psychotherapy and healing work as well as spiritual development, as it assists in the disorganization of the defensive isolated self and facilitates the experience of space and emptiness (as a prelude to the development of new connections to the world).[2] In some of the older spiritual traditions emptiness of mind was the goal of spiritual life. In the process of change described in this book, formlessness is developed by asking and holding questions, by allowing oneself to be impacted by the world, and by developing behaviors that allow change to be a part of life. Fluidity of connection is emphasized over emptiness of mind, but the cultivation of formlessness is still the energetic basis for changes in the self.

Seeking Deeper Connections

The pursuit of deeper internal and external connections is another way in which formlessness enters the spiritual process. This can be a major focus of psychospiritual development—seeking more depth in the connection to self and to others, and adding more spiritual dimensions to one's life. If I seek a deeper connection to God, to Nature, to other aspects of myself, or to others, I must also face the question of **how** I am connecting. Do I wish to control the way my spirituality develops or can I trust its emergence? Do I want my deepening connection to God to look and feel a certain way? Do I want to be dependent or feel more taken care of? To use or be used? To possess and control my spiritual experience? What are my attitudes and how open am I to being touched in turn by these experiences and energies? The willingness to be open to what occurs both inwardly and in my experience of others means that I am able to bring formlessness into the process—it means that I do not control what happens when I reach out and I can allow myself to change in the process as well. I must be able *to blend*, not control, and to do so I must reach from the question and be in the question as the process continues.

The term *blending* describes the experience of touching some other energy (such as another person, a structure in nature, or an aspect of self) with no need to exert control over the process. It describes the possibility of being moved or changed by something we connect to without losing our own identity or interfering with the identity of the other. To be touched by someone means that I allow myself to have a reaction to him or her. To blend with another means that I participate in the connection and my own movement becomes an important part of the contact.

Blending describes connection without possession, without judgment, and without merging. When a mother blends with her child, she sees and acknowledges its own needs and identity as well as her own. She gives care within a framework of respect for the identity of the child and supports his or her emerging expressions. When we involve ourselves with the earth or with other people, blending differentiates itself from possession and control in that no attempt is made to change the nature of the other while contact is held. **This way of connecting requires a tolerance and celebration of formlessness, since the outcome is always a question.** If I focus my attention on how I am responding rather than trying to control the other's response, I am struggling with the blending process rather than possession. I am in the question about my emerging identity and the outcome of the contact. **Deepening contact with any living form means a constant shift in the self experience.**

The Dark Night of the Soul

There are phases in the psychospiritual process in which the individual *loses previous knowledge and connection* and undergoes a dark time of anguish, despair, and loneliness. This experience, known generically as the Dark Night of the Soul, has been described as an aspect of psychospiritual development in Christian mysticism, the journey out of addiction, the Vietnam War combat experience, and as a contemporary experience in the journey of many people toward personal realization. The loss of connection to healthy parts of the self, to sources of inner strength and wisdom, or to God and one's spiritual world, can be among the most painful and frightening parts of a psychospiritual crisis.

Writers in the field of spiritual development have distinguished between two different levels of this process of loss of connection—the *Dark Night of the Ego* and the *Dark Night of the Soul* (see Bragdon, 1990). In the first experience, the individual loses the familiar connection with personal identity as defensive structures dissolve and a deeper personal essence emerges. This level of purification involves the personality and the question "Am I something deeper than ego?" The Dark Night of the Soul is a more extensive process of purification involving the quality of the soul. What had previously been a constant and faithful connection to the Godhead becomes broken in the purification process.

> This, precisely, then, is what the divine ray of contemplation does. In striking the soul with its divine light, it surpasses the natural light and thereby darkens and deprives individuals of all the natural affections and apprehensions

they perceive by means of their natural light. It leaves their spiritual and natural faculties not only in darkness but in emptiness too. Leaving the soul thus empty and dark, the ray purges and illumines it with divine spiritual light, while the soul thinks it has no light and that it is in darkness. (St. John of the Cross, 1979)

The loss of previous knowledge, whether personal or spiritual, is an entry into formlessness of the most difficult kind. Previous answers that represented the foundation of one's faith in oneself or one's spiritual life no longer exist. The questions, "Who am I? Is there a God? or Do I have a soul?" challenge the fundamental assumptions of one's existence and psychospiritual identity. Walking through periods of formlessness like these test many previously formed structures of connection built on faith, grace, and forgiveness.

Embracing Mystery

The movement of consciousness beyond the local self (i.e., the personal contents of the mind or the experience of the body) into the larger spiritual universe requires a shift in thinking as well as more fluid movements of the energies of the body. In contemporary Western spirituality there are many ways to challenge the bodymind to embrace larger visions of reality. Examples include:

•working with subtle energetic flows in and around the body—the Oriental traditions of QiGong; the microcosmic orbit and the organic flows of Mantak Chia; the Kundalini and pranayama breath work of the Yogas; and the energy exercises of many different spiritual schools;
•archetypal energy bands—working with the images and rituals of gods and goddesses; sensing larger patterns of energy within the self that direct choice and

purpose;

•mediumship—allowing the physical body to be a transmitter of different consciousness patterns and energy flows for the purpose of healing and spiritual education;

•earth religions and the nature forms—blending with the energies of the planetary rhythms, the seasons, the natural forms that have inhabited this planet, the Mother and Father essences;

•core energy flows associated with the emotional body in spiritual work—blending with the essential state energies like compassion or courage;

•mystical traditions of eastern and western spirituality—the development of prayer and meditative practices;

•logos experiences—touching sources of scientific and spiritual knowledge; or,

•embracing soulness—cultivating the experience of one's individual soul and higher- self expressions and bringing them through the body. The expression of one's personal purpose and spiritual lifestyle.

Each of these is an aspect of some spiritual discipline that emphasizes living in the question and embracing the mystery of the universe. These connections require the blendings of self and universe that create new self structures. Each of these practices allows one to open to questions of identity and put former answers up for examination. These practices put the experience and definition of the self at risk in that each connection made will have an unpredictable impact on self experience and touch parts of the self previously unknown. In their individual spiritual disciplines, most people touch such a small part of the larger order that mystery and surprise come to be a fundamental part of expanded consciousness. Knowing a universe that is being created in the moment is the essence of the formlessness experience.

In that universe, there are many more questions than answers. Any answer only lasts a moment and the next connection is another question.

The connection with formlessness in spiritual life is beautifully described in this passage by Evelyn Underhill (Underhill, 1942):

> To "look with the eyes of love" seems a vague and senti-mental recommendation: yet the whole art of spiritual com-munion is summed in it, and exact and important results flow from this exercise. The attitude which it involves is an attitude of complete humility and of receptiveness; with-out criticism, without clever analysis of the thing seen. When you look thus, you surrender your I-hood; see things at last as the artist does; for their sake, not for your own. The fundamental unity that is in you reaches out to the unity that is in them; and you achieve the "Simple Vision" of the poet and the mystic—that synthetic and undistorted appre-ciation of things which is the antithesis of the single vision of practical man.

Another description of the surrender to formlessness is given in this passage by Irina Tweedie (Tweedie, 1979):

> I said to him, "Our relationship to God is something en-tirely different from what we usually imagine it to be. We think that the relationship of God and Man is a duality. But it is not so. I have found that our relationship to God is something quite different. It is a merging, without words, without thought even; into 'something.' Something so tre-mendous, so endless, merging in Infinite Love, physical body and all, disappearing in it. And the physical body is under suffering; it is taut like a string in this process of an-nihilation. This is our experience of God and it cannot be otherwise.

Spiritual life always involves the encounter of formlessness and form. Our forms touch formlessness and are changed in the process. The soul (and other as-pects of the spiritual self) holds the possibilities of what we can create, and the body must stretch and expand to give those possibilities expression.

Forms of Formlessness

In this chapter I have tried to share some of the flavor of the formlessness experience. Its nature is to change and be different—for everyone and over time. It is like staring into the reaches of space around the planet. For some, it is the clear, empty experience of the boundless oceans of life. For others, it is like seeing clouds form, disintegrate, and reform into other shapes. For some, the dark spaces seem cold, empty, and frightening. For others, the emptiness is full of life and the chaos is only temporary. We pass from one to the other of these experiences—from chaos into questions; from control into surrender; from not knowing to direct knowledge; from tentative experimentation to confident expression. Each of these experiences is a struggle to control and have answers and each is an opportunity to be fluid and form more of a self. These experiences of formlessness are only way-stations, lessons to learn about reality, and experiences to walk in and through. Formlessness is multidimensional, abstract and complex, fluid and changing, full of light and sound. It is up to us as we touch it to bring forth structures in that space that allow connection to the potential it contains.

.

Chapter 3

The Formula for Change

*The Formula for Change describes the process
by which the experience of formlessness
enters consciousness and begins to
work in facilitating healing and
the expansion of the self
experience.*

S imply stated, the primary goals of personal growth work are to enhance the ability of the individual to move and to change (i.e., to create movement in the bodymind by "setting things in motion," physically, emotionally, and energetically) and to expand the capacity of the person to connect with choice to more parts of him- or herself and the world. Over time, this process has periods of steady growth, periods of stagnation, and times when it occurs as an intense and explosive experience. Health and wholeness are not static states and balance is not necessarily a state of calmness. The ability to change means that we are impacted by the experiences we have—that our need to control the outside world becomes less and our capacities to respond in healthy ways to a wide variety of energies increases. Change also means that new aspects of self-consciousness and self-expression emerge and we become more multidimensional—that we continue, in our own individual ways, to form more and deeper connections with body and earth and with soul and universe.

The Formula for Change

Earlier discussions emphasized that the experience of formlessness always accompanies the process of change. In fact, it is the initial outcome of any changes that occur in the internal structures of the mind or body. Destruction and disorganization are necessary so that new processes and structures can arise. Old behaviors, belief systems, and attitudes have to go to make room for new choices. One of the models that does an excellent job describing the various phases of the change process is known as the **Formula for Change**[1] and a discussion of this model will help illustrate how formlessness enters the change process and how structural changes in the self experience occur.

In its simplest form, this model has four stages:

Acceptance
Responsibility
Release
Change

or, phrased in terms of working with questions and answers:

Acceptance:
Seeing and Knowing the Problem
Responsibility:
Asking the Question
Release:
The Ability to Receive the Answer

Change:
The Ability to Use (move with) the Answer

Each of these phases describes a different way of using energy for problem solving and personal change, beginning with the process of seeing and knowing the problem, then examining our willingness to change, bringing the old structures into consciousness and experiencing their dissolution, working with formlessness, and finally bringing in the questions and information necessary to make a new choice or solve the problem. It also emphasizes that the process of personal and spiritual change is a **problem-solving process, an active experience in seeking truth, asking questions, being open to all answers, and actively doing the answer once received.**

Acceptance

The first step in solving problems is knowing what they are, and the basic meaning of acceptance is to see and to know a problem—to **name** it. It is not possible to make any kind of change if the problem is not accessible to consciousness. So the first step in any change process is to bring the state or the energy or the behavioral pattern into conscious awareness. Acceptance requires the development of the witness and the observer. Acceptance grows as levels of awareness and self-knowledge increase.

The cultivation of acceptance begins a process of "knowing." This process is often larger than just the gathering of information. Implied in the term *acceptance* is the knowing that involves both the mind and the heart—both knowing rationally with the faculties of the senses and thought processes **and** the intuitive knowing of the world that comes with direct experience. Acceptance of the world or some part of the self means that we contact it both symbolically and directly—that we name, see, feel, and touch the experience, and move toward it in a way that alters our being and expands our consciousness. The term *direct intuitive insight* describes this knowing process of the heart, and working with the process of acceptance aids in the development of these abilities.

It follows from this description that acceptance is first and foremost a perception, and is not a decision about what is right and what is wrong; not a process of agreeing or disagreeing with what is seen; and not a reaction to the event or the energy. **It means bringing one's attention to a problem with the intent to know the truth involved.** Acceptance means developing honesty and looking at things non-judgementally without making demands about how things ought to be.

Making a judgment about something brings a filter to the perception and stops change from occurring. Making something bad or wrong or even right or good makes it **an answer** (i.e., forms it up too quickly) and erases the opportunity for formlessness to enter the process. Thus shame, blame, and guilt—all judgments about one's self or another's experience—become major impediments to acceptance. These ego states hold us to some past, fixed way of looking at the experience. They fix the nature of the experience in time and render it rigid. They make a closed boundary between the person judging and the person encountered, thus stopping connection. There are many forms that judgments take. For example:

- blaming someone for whatever you are feeling
- making yourself wrong for your feelings
- striving to be always right in discussions
- feeling guilt over an action that you did
- carrying resentment over some past wrongs done to you

•feeling better than, more than, or less than someone else
  •shame is a judgment
  •rage and anger can contain judgment
  •disconnecting , going into isolation, or becoming objective about something is often done in judgment

These judgments are the opposite of looking at something with "a beginner's mind" and being open to new possibilities. To change something requires that the outcome be left in the question; to see what the problem is requires the attitude of acceptance.

There are some other attitudes that acceptance **is not**. Acceptance is not a passive state, like resignation might be. It is not reactive; it does not separate and take the person away from the event being observed. Acceptance brings with it a way of touching something so that it can be known, a kind of hello in which in that moment all that you are, and all that the thing being observed is, can both exist at the same time.

Acceptance is also not associated with or limited by any particular emotional state. However, it is not necessarily emotionally neutral either. For example, it can be extremely kind and loving when it is a part of the experience of compassion. Since acceptance involves the heart, almost any feeling can accompany the knowing experience, so long as the feeling state is accompanied by a willingness to make a connection. Thus I can be angry at you and be in isolation, or I can be angry and still be accepting of your feelings. If I am willing to make a connection to you with my anger and still allow you to be in your feelings, I have blended anger with acceptance. Humor is another emotional expression that supports acceptance. Humor is a way of lightening the energies of startle, fear, pain, anger, or distress. It can bring movement when we are tending toward freezing or depression. It can help us see two sides when we were only seeing one. The emotional states that do interfere with acceptance are those that express judgment about, separation from, and control over what others might be experiencing.

In addition to having feeling states as a part of the experience of acceptance, the acceptance of a problem or a situation can certainly *result* in many different feelings. One reason it is so difficult to accept many situations is that to do so would have us feel very deeply. The remorse in seeing how we have hurt someone, the grief in knowing something is over, or the anger that can come when we acknowledge that we are being hurt, are sometimes the outcome of working with acceptance. The struggle to accept such situations means opening the heart to more intense emotional experiences.

As the development of acceptance continues, it forms the basis of further expansions into states of caring, compassion, kindness, and love. These states require even more development of the heart, and are necessary for blending with the dark and wounded parts of the self. Many self structures, especially those wrapped in childhood pain and neglect, will not move much if only touched in neutrality. They require a caring and compassionate touch to come into consciousness and be released.

Acceptance is the initial phase of the change process that brings consciousness to the problem (or the self or the body). As such, it serves as the first step in integration. It is also the initial step in creating connections to others in the process known as **blending.** Anything touched by acceptance also contains the possibility of being changed by that connection. Acceptance brings energies together and forms a temporary bond that can grow in any direction. It is the beginning of forming the witness function of the ego and establishing healthy structures for exploring the self. If you can help a person establish a field of acceptance around whatever it is that he or she wishes to change, you have helped that person enormously in beginning a healing. The formlessness that occurs with the acceptance process allows other parts of the self to emerge and reinforces a healthy movement toward problem solving.

Naming

There is one facet of the acceptance process that has received much attention in psychology, and when used correctly, can be a major tool in facilitating change. This is the process of **naming.** Most scientific efforts regard this as a first step in understanding any phenomena—to get a good description of the pattern or the structure of a thing before making any explanations about it or trying to change anything. In psychology, the naming process has been called the Rumplestiltskin effect, after the fairy tale, and refers to the seemingly magical effects that can come from helping an individual find a name for something that has not been a part of his or her reality. The naming of something involves bringing the nature of that structure into conscious awareness. The process can run the gamut from diagnosing an illness, divulging a secret, opening a new reality (like the psychic world) to a person, identifying a painful or dysfunctional belief, naming a behavioral pattern, or calling a lie. In many circumstances, this process can be a powerful emotional experience. One's reality changes as hidden structures come to the light of consciousness. In olden times, when dragons and wizards possessed the original names for things, they had control over them, and the name for the thing contained within it something of its essence. It was the "truth" of the object, and power over the object came through knowing the sound (the energy equation) of the name. In the psychological arena, the naming of something still possesses that power. If you speak someone's truth, with the correct name and/or energy, whether it be negative or positive, you stir up something deep in the body and psyche and there is a **resonance**. Things change. Structures become visible, known, and conscious and then require integration into the identity and behavior. If that integration and owning of the structure cannot be done by the person who was named, whoever "sees" the condition has the power. For example, if I name someone's behavioral game, or point out an unconscious pattern, or reveal a secret being hidden, I temporarily have a kind of power over that person. By doing the naming, I put her or him in reaction to me.[2] I am in charge of his or her process for a time, since I have highlighted a structure that was not part of his or her conscious reality, or was one that he or she preferred to keep hidden. **I have forced this person to move either toward or away from the name—to either meet the name with acceptance, or to defend, reject, and separate from the experience. I have changed their timing and influenced their acceptance of the experience.** This powerful process can be used for healing or for destructive ends; I have seen both in therapeutic and political arenas.

There are enormous healing benefits in helping an individual bring his or her strengths to conscious awareness. Also, great relief follows when a healer diagnoses a medical or psychological condition and someone "knows" (i.e., might have power over) the state. Much of the cultural power that physicians, psychologists, and other healers have comes from their ability to name the reality (the illness or imbalance) of the patient and provide some methods for changing the condition. However, the individual must also commit to the process (and the name) if healing is to be more than symptom relief. The individual must let him- or herself be touched by the name—move toward it and thus change. The first step in that process is bringing in the energy of acceptance. Doing the naming with judgment, and not with acceptance, or with the need to manipulate or control the individual, works to strengthen the defenses and move the individual away from formlessness and healing[3]. Instead of opening to questions, the individual moves back into answers, defenses, and protective responses. If done in a negative way, it can be virtually impossible for the person to bring the structures into consciousness at a later time.

If I am the therapist or the physician, I have the responsibility to do the naming in such a way as to make it a healing (a choiceful) and not a shaming (or avoidant) experience. I cannot take away the client's right to question and react. In therapy and psychospiritual work, these are extremely subtle processes and it is important that fields of acceptance be around all interactions in which the individual is exploring areas of pain, shame, secrets, or the dark side[4]. In therapy, an individual's timing and his or her ability to organize around the named material and use the support available are important considerations. If at all possible, an individual should name (be helped to explore and question) his or her own patterns and thus stay sovereign to the process of opening up into formlessness.

Responsibility

Taking responsibility for a problem is the second stage in the process of moving toward a solution. This is the stage in which you ask questions. How do I solve this problem? What can I do? How much of this problem is mine? What did I do here to create this problem? What can I change here? Taking responsibility moves you one step further toward the structure that you wish to change—but it is a moving toward that involves **asking questions** rather than being in judgment or trying to establish right or wrong.

In the stage of responsibility, an individual says neither, "It's your fault that I feel this way," nor, "It's all my fault and I'm wrong." As with the acceptance phase, one must continue to stay out of judgment about a problem or an aspect of the self, and instead look at it and ask questions. Where am I involved here? Where do I contribute to the problem? How do I maintain this situation with my agreement or my contribution? The important difference between making a judgment and taking responsibility is that being responsible for a problem requires acceptance in order to see one's involvement clearly. We have moved into judgment when shame, or its projection, blame, becomes attached to the perception. At this point the movement toward a solution gets stopped. A fine line exists between being responsible for a problem and making judgments about our participation, but further exploration will often reveal levels of shame or guilt attached to our inability to immediately create a solution. Accepting responsibility means that we can be in present time about a problem and not be encumbered with structures from the past, including blame, shame, and guilt.

It follows, then, that the stage of responsibility is the stage in the change process where there is still further separation from the problem by the **appropriate assignment of causation**. In healing work, it means the inner child is able to see that he or she was not at fault, and discover that he or she may have merged with the perpetrator or taken in the negative beliefs of the environment. In the responsibility stage all the issues of sovereignty, autonomy, blame, separation, and possession are faced in order to discover the inner self-movement. This is the stage in change where one says no to patterns that are no longer working and makes choices to create new self-movements instead of using the old solutions or the solutions of others. Once these issues are faced, the healing process can proceed to the next stage, in which the emotional pain can be released and new solutions can be developed.

One of the spiritual principles relevant to the phase

of taking responsibility for our problems and solutions is the idea that we create our own reality. There are many levels of interpretation and truth embedded in this maxim. As personal consciousness expands, people keep discovering the many ways it is true. Realizing how much we create our reality by the belief systems we hold (and the way in which these beliefs immediately label and structure our experience) is one of the fruits of personal exploration. However, this principle does not imply that we have directly invited all the events that impinge on us, or that there are no independently moving forces in the universe that might cross our paths. So if we get hit by a car, struck by lightning, get ill, or experience misfortune, the first response need not be to assign blame or self-causation, but rather to examine the situation with acceptance in order to see what is involved. Responsibility means looking at how we might have been involved and what levels of choice we did have, and then establishing that we are active participants in how we choose to respond. Taking responsibility means that we ask questions about our involvement in (or how we touch) structures, **not** that we establish fault. Responsibility moves us toward **participation and connection in present time**. We are looking for information about how to respond differently, how to change within ourselves, and how to make choices—not how to account for everything that impacts us. Living in the Question with regard to acceptance and responsibility means that the individual is able to ask, "How might I see the problem more clearly, so I can have more choice about how to respond?"

This **responsibility** stage of change goes deep into issues regarding how well we care for ourselves and how well we take responsibility for the different aspects of our lives. There are many impediments to negotiating this stage. Most people have problem areas in which they have felt victimized and have given up any hope of change or finding a solution. Acknowledging "I don't know what I can do" might be the only step possible at first, but if it is done with acceptance instead of judgment, the next step—asking "What part of it can I change?"—becomes more possible.

If the field of acceptance is the willingness to see and know the truth of a problem, then the field of responsibility is the willingness to move forward into seeing your involvement and the willingness to bring in conscious choice. It is the willingness to move toward the problem named and accepted. In that way, responsibility is a further movement toward formlessness, an opportunity to become aware of where you have touched others and a willingness to know the nature of that connection. Acceptance and responsiblity involve allowing yourself to be touched by your problems, your issues, and the energies that fill your world. Allowing your world to touch your core is at the heart of these phases of the change cycle[5].

At a workshop I attended, I came across this statement a psychologist used to help his clients manage their chronic pain experience[6]. It is an excellent description of moving into acceptance and responsibility around a difficult issue:

I Have a Condition

I have a condition in my life called _____.
And while it is not a condition that I like, it is one that I have. However, I have something to say about how I am being in regard to my condition. What I have to say is: There is more to me than the condition and I am therefore not the condition. I am bigger than the condition because I have it rather than it having me. I manage the condition rather than its managing me, and it is I, rather than the condition, who run and control my life. I can have it as a problem to hate, fight, and resist, or not, and that is my choice. I choose not to have it as a problem to hate, fight, and resist but instead to let it be, and

to take effective and appropriate action in regard to it—
whatever that may be.

Release

The word *release* is a bit of a misnomer for this next stage of change, since release is not the only process involved. This stage of change also involves the ability to **receive an answer,** and this process is often dependent on letting the old solutions release their hold on our consciousness. Changing self structures involves both bringing the lies up into consciousness and allowing new solutions and potential choices to emerge. If, in the earlier stages of the process, the fields of acceptance and responsibility have been opened, then you have already asked questions about what choices to make and/or actions to take. The next step involves being open to receiving this information. This is much easier said than done, since existing defensive structures of the self have strong needs to be in control of how much change occurs. Also, most of us are very partial to prior answers—those familiar solutions that worked, at least partially, in the past. Most often we want to **control** what we will become if we are changing. Receiving an answer is fundamentally a process of giving up control—or better, moving the **locus of control** to different (and perhaps yet unknown) structures within the psyche. Enabling your answers or your wisdom to emerge from these other sources is a further move toward allowing formlessness and a further opening to touching other parts of the self.

The stage of **release,** then, is the process by which new questions and answers come into consciousness—the ways in which we let go of old answers/lies/solutions/repetitive patterns and make a step toward our intuition/our inner voices/our "guides"/and the structures of our healthy side. The release stage generally has three aspects to it: (1) a stage of disorganization that I am calling **creative disorganization**; (2) an opportunity to experience and accept formlesness; and (3) a stage in which new answers are received, metabolized, and accepted. There may also be a change in the locus of control from external or defensive structures inward to other aspects of the self. In most individuals these occur almost at the same time. The old experience of the self changes, feelings come up, new questions get asked, and new answers or other ways of thinking or acting emerge. There is no average time period for this process and its progress is dependent mostly on how much consciousness is present, how much support is available, and how many skills in problem solving the individual has developed.

Creative Disorganization

In the stages of acceptance and responsibility, the individual seeks to touch and know the problem and accepts responsibility for shaping a response to that problem. The next step in the process (release) involves letting go of old self structures that would interfere with change. When an individual comes in for therapy or begins a personal growth process, this person soon becomes aware that he or she has a number of patterns of behavior, including beliefs about the self, that were formed in childhood and persist into adulthood. Many of these patterns and beliefs are "defensive" in nature—that is, they are learned patterns of behavior that were originally designed to ward off emotional pain. They were the responses of a child subjected to trauma, neglect, or other forms of abuse who needed to diminish the impact of those experiences. Going numb, closing down and hiding, never reaching out again, and becoming aggressive are examples of such patterns. Each of these structures formed around trauma carries with it a definition of self or a belief system about the self that often is negative and extremely limiting to adult development[7]. The other main category of responses includes patterns of behavior orginally formed because the child was told that it was good or better to be a certain way, and the caregivers reinforced her or him for carrying on in those patterns. These behaviors almost always reflect the basic belief systems of the family system. Examples include, "Don't ask, don't feel, don't cry, be strong"; "To be good is to be silent about your pain"; "To work as hard as possible is good"; "Parents sacrifice for their children"; "Don't elevate yourself too much"; and so on. In all of these examples, a "self" gets formed and reinforced without much witness or examination. Because the behaviors worked early on, the child assumes they will work in the future. These patterns defy change in adulthood because they did have some success at first, even if the cost was further development. They become the basis of a personality and a set of patterns and beliefs about the self that only come up for examination when they cease to work in current time. They cease to work when the consequence for maintaining the patterns is loss of intimacy in the present and when they limit further development of the self.

Each repetitive pattern in the personality operates like a machine. The bodymind learns these programs and runs them off in the presence of the appropriate stimuli or whenever a certain state of consciousness is dominant. These mechanisms allow behavior patterns to be efficient, automatic, and stable. We do not have to examine each movement to see if it applies to the current situation, and we can engage in complex sequences of acts (like driving a car, or playing a role) without obsessing over each component. These same mechanisms, however, may not serve us well when they involve interactions with other people or situations whose characteristics change and require different responses. When such behaviors become automatic and unexamined, they turn into *rituals* and cease to reflect the needs of the situation or the potential of the individuals involved. If their origin was defensive in nature, they can be very reactive/protective and are only in the best interest of one individual. For example, to react to people as if their requests represent demands, or to always "know what's best" for a child, are ritualistic ways of connecting to others. These patterns, first learned as protections, may in present time destroy intimacy. Rituals almost always reflect stagnation in a system. While they might have begun as positive responses to a situation, eventually they become harmful.

Each ritual, especially those that involve connection to other people, carries with it a belief system about the self and the world, a set of expectations, a set of feeling states, and a set of action patterns. A ritual is a state of consciousness that contains a particular answer. Each time we do not have a new solution to a problem that persists, we reinforce the position that we are the same and that the world is the same, and we miss the fact that the world has changed and that we, as well, have learned something in the meantime. Repeating beliefs about the self reinforces stagnation and solidity and excludes formlessness. The release phase of the change process involves the examination and release of old rituals of behavior regarding others and, along with those, the letting go of old structures that define the self.

The release phase of the change process also involves touching the emotional pain and expressions of feeling that were blocked by judgments and the defenses that were erected for survival. Release is a potent and purifying aspect of the personal change experience. As the old solutions and answers become less dominant, new solutions are allowed to come forward. Healing forces, more adaptive ways of looking at problems, and the many levels of creative wisdom and expression within the self can emerge. New life can be expressed and cultivated. These expressions of new self-organizations reflect the operation of the healing energies that lie within the self.

The Emergence of Formlessness

It is during the release phase that the experience of formlessness becomes most salient. In letting go of old self structures and answers, an individual will also encounter voids in the personality, experiences of chaos, and all of the feelings and behaviors inherent in the early formation of these structures. Letting go of any of these ritualistic behaviors results in a change in one's identity. What will happen if I can't control how people feel about me? How will I protect myself if I give up my anger? What will I be like when I am no longer a caretaker? Will I die or go crazy if all of my feelings come up? What will fill up the gaps if I let go of some part of me? Many questions and few answers characterize the release phase of changing. The individual must search and listen for new answers and make choices about which ones to use. The experience of formlessness can take many forms as the reorganization of the self continues.

In the next two chapters, I will spend more time discussing the entire process of creative disorganization and the ways in which formlessness shifts the locus of control toward deeper parts of the self. Next is a description of the phase of the change process that involves **reorganizing the self experience.**

Change

In the final stage of the formula for change, the term *change* refers to the behaviors involved in **acting on the answer**; that is, moving the process out further toward interaction with the world. Just knowing the answer is not enough. No change is complete unless the process involves acting and doing. Actually, not many answers reveal themselves in full form anyway. The doing stage is the test ground for what feels right and for what works. When it comes to the development of the self, we **discover and develop** our answers by trial and error more often than not, rather than just "know them" in full form. We often get only a piece of the process at a time, and must act on that piece to get the rest.

"Change" as a stage in the formula as a whole refers to the steps people take as they reorganize their self-concept and recreate the ways they connect to the external world. It refers to the process by which an individual integrates formlessness into the change experience and how she or he is able to use questions as starting points for further development. Acting from an energy like formlessness requires making choices, since most questions have several answers and there is no "right" one except by trying it out and seeing what happens. One of the best metaphors I have heard for this aspect of changing compares the process to walking on a balance beam in complete darkness. You take a step and find out where your foot lands. If it does not feel solid, you change direction. If it hits solid ground, you proceed. The solidness of the ground in this example is when there is some expression of yourself that feels satisfying, that promotes life in yourself and others, and that deepens the connection to aspects of yourself or to the external world. One of the skills developed in psychospiritual work is a "knowing" about when this is occurring and making more choices in those directions. This experience of beginning to know the self by a procedure of trial and error in connecting to the world also reflects something of the structure of the "self" itself. The essence of this process is not to discover some hidden form that lies below or outside of consciousness, but to actually create the form of the self by our choices and actions. The process is soul-making at its core. Not soul-discovering, but soul-**making.** The body, as the vehicle of action, creates the forms by which the soul comes into the physical world and shows the nature of the personal essence.

The change phase also involves becoming conscious of one's inability to move. In this phase the individual learns to work with exhaustion, passivity, immobilization, and the tendency to isolate and stay disconnected. Learned helplessness is a powerful force in keeping people stuck, as are those aspects of depression and fear that prevent movement toward others. Change requires skills in accessing will and engaging in movement. Formlessness means "living in the question," and "living" requires multidimensional movement.

In Chapter 7 there is further discussion of the reorganization process. The final goal of the Formula for Change is to bring choice into the development of self and to enhance that self by connection to the external world.

As a description of the process of change, the Formula for Change reflects a fluid process—not always occurring in linear steps or with clearly defined sections. When you look at how people actually change in life, you see that it is a fluid process, with spontaneous, non-linear leaps intermixed with long stagnant periods of hard conscious work. Change is a pulsation, where connections to the world are brought into our core and new responses are organized that deepen that connection. The steps in the Formula are best seen in the slower times, when specific stages need specific attention and the application of the Formula in a conscious way is helpful. Those times of grace when we see a problem, accept it, and can let go of the old answer and implement a new solution all in one breath do occur sometimes, but are more rare than the steady application of our consciousness to problem areas. The Formula for Change is most often a kind of helix or spiral—a piece of the problem is tackled, worked through, changed, and a larger piece can

then be taken on. Again and again we approach the issue until we can look back and see how much has actually changed and how we have changed in the process.

In summary, the Formula for Change describes the
way in which the experience of formlessness enters the
structures of the psyche. It describes how we bring our
awareness (the witness function) into psychological and
behavioral structures that previously existed in isolation
(without the potential to change and develop), and how
we can create more diverse connections to the world
based on our increasing consciousness.

Chapter 4

Light and Darkness

*Dark side or unhealthy side structures provide the most
resistance to change. They have the least
amount of formlessness in them; prefer the
most secrecy; have the most judgment
in them; were mostly organized
around protection, possession,
or control; and are networked
with the most painful and
negative emotional states.*

As part of the general question of what gets disorganized in the change process (in order to be more in the question), we can look once more at which self structures actually change in psychospiritual development. What would be the reason for disorganization and what would make it a healthy or unhealthy process? Why should something come apart? Why can't you just add new thoughts, feelings, or beliefs and let the old ones decay from disuse? These are very useful questions, since many spiritual development approaches strongly advocate emphasizing the good or the positive to the exclusion of directly experiencing and working other sides of the personality, such as the shadow and the darker structures in the psyche[1]. Such approaches have recommended strategies like "don't think about it" or "emphasize only love" when patterns of negativity emerge. In recent years, however, much attention has been focused on working with the shadow side of life, and there is a growing consensus that significant shifts in the structure of the self experience require facing the dark side (Zweig and Abrams, 1991). Certainly people can and do make big changes from only adding healthy structures to the self. Such additions are necessary for healing to occur and they form the basis for further spiritual growth. However, these same additions also highlight what has not been touched. As your light shines brighter, it cannot help turning toward the inside of you, revealing what is hidden, and what is not able to change. The dark side of the personality will emerge with continued growth, because that is what the transformation process requires—a breakdown of boundaries between inner and outer reality and the subdivisions of the self. There are other reasons as well, but to elaborate on them requires making some distinctions between the different terms used to describe these phenomena. There are three different concepts that I will use in this discussion:

> The Shadow
> The Healthy Sides of the Personality
> The Unhealthy or Dark Side

The term *shadow* denotes unconsciousness—those energies and structural formations of the psyche that operate outside of awareness. Facing your shadow means bringing light to those structures—the intentions they contain and the emotions held in them. Many levels of psychological functioning occur in the shadow and they can be both healthy and unhealthy, constructive and destructive. Not everything unconscious is bad for you, and many forms of emotions as well as spiritual energies move through people but remain unconscious to present-time awareness. Complex structures of the self can be part of the shadow (like archetypal formations) and be determinants of significant behavioral patterns and resonances to external events. To bring such structures "out of the shadow" brings them into consciousness and they can be more readily expressed with choice and even further developed for the benefit of the individual or group.

The other set of terms, and the ones most important to this chapter, are the *healthy side* and *unhealthy (Dark) sides* of each person. These mean something different from the term *shadow*. In the Teacher's process, one important observation was how psychospiritual development proceeds when there are two things happening: First, work was done on strengthening those parts of the self that support change, connection, and movement. Second, equally powerful work was done focusing on those belief systems, those stagnant and dead states, and those mental, physical, and emotional structures that **avoid or prevent** the process of movement and connection. Within the self there are both healthy and unhealthy structures.

The Healthy Side

Let us again consider the idea discussed in Chapter 1—that the self experience is based on a variety of psychophysical structures or ego states coexisting in more or less harmony or conflict. That is, upon examination we find many different self structures, some so developed that they are like "selves" or subpersonalities, each such network having a set of beliefs, abilities, reaction patterns, goals, and needs. Some of these "selves" can be quite creative, fluid, and changing—like the ways in which an individual develops as a businessperson, athlete, gardener, healer, artist, mystic, or teacher. Many of these developed self structures foster creative connection with the world and grow more complex over time. Other self structures can promote isolation and avoidance of contact, be more or less unconscious, and be quite fixed in their expression—like some parts of the "wounded child" structures that are defensive and reactive. Some "selves" are very transient, like certain bodymind states an individual might use in creative or spiritual work, while others are more permanent and seem like the usual personality of the individual. However developed, these self structures are the ways people connect to the world, and they serve as channels for the energies and purposes deeper within. With work, most people can become aware of these "experienced selves" and begin to bring more choice into their expression— that is, use the energies and the abilities inherent in the structures and begin to move into them with more choice.

As I mentioned in Chapter 1, the idea of "multiplicity of selves" as the basic structure of the personal self also brings with it a different idea of psychological health. Health is present when the individual has the ability to choicefully shift between these different states and selves, and when they are co-conscious—that is, the selves know about each other and the purpose each serves. Distress and suffering occur when there is no flexibility in the ego states to meet the requirements of current problems and when there is no choice or awareness about what is being expressed. Since life seems to continuously demand lots more choice and a lot more fluidity than most of us are able to generate on short notice, people who wish to change are mostly working on the edges of their consciousness and on what they are able to embrace as self. In other words, they are stretching to allow increasingly different states of consciousness and expression to emerge.

Health, then, means that we are developing the ability to move between and among states and structures, and learning to make choices about how to act in the different states. It means that I am better able to move between focused states of creative production to open states of reflection; between alert arousal and relaxed being; between giving help and receiving nurturance; between being emotionally grounded in my body and in contact with other dimensions of time and space. It also means that in the midst of a contraction into anxiety or rage I can feel what I am doing and make some choice about what to do next. As health and awareness increase, each structure (each way of being) that emerges has the possibility of more connection to the external world and this brings more of the potentials within the person out as well. As formlessness enters the process of change, the likelihood increases that the rigid defensive structures coming into consciousness will begin disorganizing, and the newly created behaviors will be more in the question.

Self structures often significantly differ in the degree to which they possess and accomodate formlessness, and in the degree to which they are open to the processes of change and connection. In other words, structures differ in **permeability.** Permeability means that the bodymind state we are in can be impacted by the outside world, and we can move or change with that connection without losing our identity and choice. Contact means being willing to be touched. The essence of the contact experience is the blending process that occurs when two energy systems connect. Both are affected by the contact. I am touched by you when I have allowed your energy to come through my boundary, but I have also **reached out and participated in what was happening** so my energy blends with yours. I am changed by this, and if you have done the same, so are you. If you have given me your energetic touch without an agenda as to what I should do with it or how I should respond, than I am free to make of it what I can, and I can bring choice into my process. When your touch is gone, your energy has left and what remains is some previously unknown creation of my energy and your touch. Since healing requires our participation with outside forces, as does spiritual growth, those parts of the self that cannot or will not be affected by outside energies can slow down the healing and growth.

Permeability characterizes those parts of the self that seek contact and connection, are willing and able to change through those connections, and can still maintain individual identity. From the point of view of chaos theory, permeable bodymind structures have the characteristics of an open system. They support transformation and reorganization and allow new states of health to emerge and be maintained. For a given "self" or self structure to become more permeable, it must be willing to come out of the shadow, be willing to change (i.e., not always be right, and allow others to touch it), and actually be a chosen expression of the individual, not a structure that was some part of a possession or someone else's definition of that individual. That is, I decided what to do with the energy of our contact and did not have to do what your agenda dictated.

As one develops more and more self structures that have permeability to the external world, one's capacity to respond and/or change increases, and one's identity becomes stronger, not weaker. Such people learn to make choiceful responses to more and more different kinds of situations, and are able to work with the variety of different responses that are triggered in themselves by others. They develop the ability to trust the process of being touched without so much fear as to the outcome. They ask, "How do I want to respond?" Formlessness has entered the system. This kind of development of the self is like a purging and purification process—it challenges all the structures of the self that prefer isolation or cannot or do not wish to change and connect (incorporate others).

Permeability is the characteristic of structures that allow formlessness into their functioning. Such permeability in physical structures has been discussed in presentations of chaos theory in physics (Jantsch, 1976). These kinds of structures are called "dissipative structures" and are characteristic of open-ended physical systems—that is, systems that can exchange energy and matter with the environment. Open systems all are subject to fluctuations in their stability, whether from outside forces or internal shifts, and can incorporate moments in which they are in chaos—when the apparent order in the system has collapsed and a new higher order of complexity and energy exchange can arise out of this chaos. In the discussion here, healthy systems would be able to incorporate or handle formlessness. Instability and permeability would be qualities of a healthy state of being and would support the creation of a new level of more complex structures that could handle more diversity and change.

In addition to handling more of the experience of formlessness, healthy structures can also stay connected to unhealthy ones—that is, their level of cohesion or stability is not damaged by connecting to less fluid states. So the term *healthy* also describes parts of the self that seek and can handle (have freedom of choice about) instability while making connection. This ability to resonate to many different kinds of energies without losing self-organization allows change to occur[2].

Health does not mean better, good, nice, or accommodating. A healthy person is not one without an unhealthy side. Neither does this term imply the absence of illness or a constant show of strength. It does include the ability to be conscious of what is occurring and what one is feeling and doing; an ability to help others in areas where one is strong and reach out for help where one is not; an ability to set boundaries when necessary to protect the self but still connect to a wide variety of different energies, people, and situations; an ability to allow the world to change around oneself and be changed by those experiences; an ability to make an impact on people around oneself; and the possession of personal "depth"—knowing oneself and being able to manage both one's caring and not-so-caring sides. The term implies flexibility, the capacity to care, the ability to solve problems, creativity, and self-regulation. In other words, in a healthy person, the healthy structures are dominant most of the time, and when the unhealthy sides do emerge, the individual is able to reach out for help and utilize support to move through the process. All these characteristics have at their core the persons capacity to change in accordance with what is happening around him or her and to change in such a way as to enhance the change-potential of others. The essence of health is the presence of formlessness in the self system. This allows change to occur.

With regard to the experience of self, both permeable and nonpermeable structures exist side by side in any person—that is, I have parts of myself (self structures) that are open to change and connection and parts that are not. I embrace change and I resist it with great vigor. Both kinds of ego states exist in all individuals in varying degrees of separation and cohesion. These seemingly opposite states produce many of the struggles in the change experience, like the phenomenon of resistance in therapy, and the discovery that there are aspects of the self that pursue healing and parts that wish for self-destruction. This separation of health and unhealth within the self also means that an individual can possess good present-time information, feeling states, and behaviors that still cannot affect the structures of the dark side. Affirmation work is sometimes the victim of these separations. An individual can memorize, practice, and truly begin to believe an affirmation and yet not affect the strength of its opposite in his or her psyche. In Chapter 8, I will discuss in more detail the process of blending and some of the conditions under which health can impact unhealth to make structural shifts.

People who wish to change do not always have a very healthy side to start with. A childhood of abuse and neglect leaves its damage and the outcome is often a lack of development of healthy sides that are able to receive support, do self-care, work with feelings, and do the basic tasks important in healing. The general approach in therapeutic work with childhood trauma includes learning how to stabilize emotional states, making a connection to the therapist, and learning a number of skills to work with the painful material that will emerge. This approach addresses the need to build up sufficient healthy-side structures so healing can occur. The degree to which healthy-side structures exist in an individual also limits the depth of spiritual work one can do. Since most spiritual practices require the connection to energetic experiences that contain formlessness, there must be structures within the self that can contain energy without always triggering old and painful material. Spiritual work requires that the healing process be contained and that there be parts of the self that can solely explore health.

If there is one quality that characterizes healthy-side structures more than any other, it is their multidimensionality. This means that their range of connection is steadily increasing and the individual has the ability to connect to many different aspects of the world—physical, emotional, mental, and etheric. Healthy-side structures form containers for energies within the bodymind and bring choice to their expression. Rage can move toward anger, taking and usury can move toward longing, terror can move into fear, biting sarcasm can become more humorous, and what was unconscious can be tolerated in consciousness. Unlike most defensive dark-side structures, health has no limit to its complexity. Healthy structures of the self have a wide range of complexity and organization. They include bodymind states that tolerate the sensations and feelings of the body; that have the ability to connect to varieties of emotional states; that are able to connect to different kinds of people and their needs, and to nature and the vastness and mystery of spiritual reality. Many of these structures must be developed consciously with choice and effort, while some remain hidden and already somewhat developed in people, waiting to be opened spontaneously in moments of inspiration or need. The task of psychospiritual development is to find these spaces and structures within the self and consciously attend to their nurturing.

As I will discuss more in a later chapter, psychospiritual healing is a process in which these healthy parts of the self are brought together with the wounded sides for the express purpose of creating a third new set of structures that contain the experiences of both. This blending process, as it continues, represents the continued breaking down of boundaries between parts of the self until consciousness and choice touch all parts of the system. The dark and/or unhealthy parts of the self are **transformed** in such a process, not just defeated or sent away. The healthy parts of the self are transformed as well. Blending represents an expansion of the self experience and a lessening of constrictions. It does not mean that all these different structures of the self merge into one big blob, but it does mean that as consciousness comes into more and more parts of the self, the individual can hold the experience of multidimensionality until choices about what to do become more clear.

The Dark Side

These two different kinds of self structures, those that are permeable to change and those that are not, represent one of the fundamental splits in the self. Their coexistence seems to be a fundamental part of being human. In mythology, these two structures are represented by the forces of evil and the forces of good[3]. How they are pitted against each other within the self becomes the core of many different stories of transformation. These self structures represent two kinds of ego states with different goals, different relationships to the process of change, and different operating principles. Since spiritual development is based on the deepening of connections to self and world, these polarities of light-darkness and connection-isolation become the focus of attention in much of the work. In this essay I am using the terms *healthy side* and *dark* or *unhealthy side* to describe these two sets of structures. These terms are not value judgments and should not be applied in that way. They represent the dimension of permeability in ego structures, not *good* or *bad*. The dark or unhealthy sides of the self, in this discussion, are those structures that seek and support "darkness"—that is, isolation, disconnection, fragmentation, and **the intention to destroy connection.** The dark side of the human personality seeks to cut off and isolate from others, to judge and to control—not to seek connection and be changed by that experience. The dark side sets up and maintains walls, barriers, and differences. It seeks to maintain structure and to provide answers—to keep the truth static and unchanging rather than fluid and moving.

Figure 2 shows a general listing of the differences between the two kinds of self structures. These structures and the patterns they mediate represent very different ways of being in the world. They are not actual "selves" in most people, although in certain kinds of dissociative disorders they can seem that way. A so-called "malevolent alter"(as seen in some multiple personalities) can appear to have captured the qualities of the dark side and hold them so separate from the other parts of the self that one can see how such a structure might look. The focus is on survival, non contact through secrecy, and the willingness to hurt to defend and protect. Healthy-side structures are usually not so tightly formed; they hold a blend of many energies and appear much more fluid and complex. In most people, these two movements (connect and isolate) and the structures that mediate them are woven into the personality. When dark-side patterns are explored in self-awareness exercises, they are difficult to contact and seem to emerge separately only under conditions of stress when the healthy side is taxed, worn, challenged, or not well developed.

Just as the structures of the overall "self" in an individual are multiple, so are the structures that the unhealthy side comprises. There are at least four different kinds of self structures that support isolation and disconnection in various degrees. They can be described as follows:

- Identifications
- Defensive and protective structures
- Possession structures
- Fantasy structures

Each of these has a somewhat different origin in development and a different relationship to the individual's truth and reality. That is, they come from different sources and are more or less related to the person's own energy and choices.

Identifications are those self structures that a person has created out of his or her own experiences with other people and the world and has come to believe are synonymous with who he or she is. On the basis of my experience with my body, I might come to believe that I am not much of an athlete. It would not necessarily be a judgment, but a conclusion based on my experience with sports. I might then identify with this conclusion and act accordingly—I would not engage in sports or try to be competitive. I would self-fulfill this belief and continue to support its structure by acting in a way that did not challenge it or make it less real. It would then limit me and form a kind of bubble around which my bodily experience would continue to form. I could do the same under- or over-assessments with my intelligence, my intimacy skills, my personal value, my sexuality, and so

Healthy-Side Structures	Dark-Side Structures
Permeable to Change	**Not Willing/Able to Change**
Identifies with self as process	Identifies with self as structure
Seeks Connection	**Avoids Connection**
Goal is personal development through connection with other life. Operates in Present Time	Goal is accumulation of power through self-only development. Operates in Past Time
Inclusive	**Exclusive**
Distinguishes between boundaries and barriers	Contact is threatening to barriers and structural integrity
Creation and Destruction Occur As Aspects of Change	**Destruction Only**
Allows destruction and letting go	Connections are destroyed and control is preferred.
Invites Witness/Consciousness	**Prefers Secrecy**
Knows the difference between secrecy and privacy	Witness is threatening to the intention to control
Includes All Emotions	**Emphasis on Control**
Is willing to feel all emotions	Attempts to control what is felt—judges feelings
Acceptance	**Judgment**

Figure 2. Health and Unhealth

forth, until I had a series of structures formed that could determine who I was and could be forever. These could even be construed as my fate and I would not challenge them or notice how they might be limiting my development or forming a barrier to further movement in some arena.

Most self-identifications are of this nature—they are conclusions drawn on the basis of past experience, that limit further self-knowledge and exploration. They might be characterized by the phrase, "I like the movements I have and I do not want to give them up." Because they are formed on the basis of personal experience, they do have some truth about the person in them. The truth might be exaggerated or distorted or over- or under-emphasized, but these self-identifications do reflect the energies of the person and how he or she has lived in the world. **In this sense they can be seen as pale reflections of a deeper essence, but captured in a state of rigidity.** Sometimes they get linked to judgments and cannot develop. They are not in the question. They become issues in psychospiritual work because they are stagnant and unchanging conclusions. They become answers for all time and no further questions are asked. They lose their formlessness and become structures of the psyche that don't change until consciously challenged.

In healthy people self-identifications are the most common structures that underlie the experience of self. "That is who I am." Self-identifications possess varying degrees of permeability, connectivity, and fluidity. They have mostly been beneficial ways of coping with the struggles of life and are patterns that have by and large worked well for the individual. Identifications often feel like old friends, and there is always some loss and reluctance to letting them go. A person might *like* being right, expressing him- or herself with great drama, hoarding money, caretaking others, being self-involved, or being alone a lot. The release of those patterns so basic to the sense of self depends on seeing how they result in some harm to self or others, or how they hold back further development. Identifications can and do change slowly over a lifetime and form a level of cohesion and stability to selfhood. They are not the enemy of spiritual growth, but often form the basis of further development of health and connection. They become stretched and expanded and more permeable. Hoarding becomes the basis for the responsible use of resources and isolation develops into the appreciation of solitude. These self structures can then allow the emergence of deeper essential states of being; they become the containers for the emergence of those energies.

Protective and defensive structures are also formed on the basis of experience, but have more solidity. They are formed to prevent pain and suffering from reemerging into consciousness after having gone through that which could not be resolved or successfully processed. They state, "My own movements are difficult, painful, and frightening, so I will do something else." Defenses are the structures that keep further expressions hidden. In that sense, they do not represent truth, but hide the truth. A child usually has to handle a traumatic experience by hiding the feelings of vulnerability and pain— the truth of his or her existence in that moment of time. Defenses are formed that aid in that management process. Dissociation, denial, projection, isolation, rationalization, and so forth, all are ways that the bodymind learns to manage the experience and tries to restore the sense of safety and self-integrity necessary for survival and further growth. These movements produce isolation and separation from one's experience. At one time, defenses were necessary mechanisms for the maintenance of selfhood, and in that sense they protected life, but they do not generate life. If such structures have been around for a long time in the individual's history they become more difficult to surrender because of the "truth" they appear to represent. "If I open up I'll be hurt." "If I show you who I am, you won't like me." "It's no use to ask, nothing will come of it." These are some examples of structures that people bring into the present from the past to protect against the truth of early pain. Great harm can be perpetuated in the name of such past experiences, and defensive structures can form the basis of many unhealthy patterns.

Defenses and protections are characterized by very little formlessness. They remain surprisingly resistant to change over the years, and when they surface in consciousness work, they often have the exact form they did when first formed. They are seen in chronic tensions deep in the body, addictions that resist change, relationship patterns that persist, and attitudes that support isolation. They continue in these forms as long as they are utilized and rarely get more complex or sophisticated than they originally were. When they become more conscious and we need them less, they seem archaic and born of times past. They are the structures that support "the past that lives in the present," and the emergence out of these states represents an important breakthrough into a more present-time existence.

Possession structures are those self structures that were taught to us by others and which we took on as answers because we were not able to choose any other form. They state, "I have no movements of my own, so I will let you direct me," or, "I will take my energy and bend it to your direction." They are the connections and introjects that were not choicefully participated in and could not be met with consciousness. In the formative years of child development, the caregivers provide indormation that the child uses to form his or her behaviors. As development proceeds, maturity means that these early learnings are questioned and examined. The knowledge imparted by parental teaching is replaced by individually chosen conscious acts. If it is not, the individual remains *possessed by his or her past*. There are many levels of these influences in the psyche and they exist in the body and the mind. They range from the energies around us that came with our family unit (which we had no choice but to absorb), through those answers we were given about ourselves by others we considered authorities. Many families have levels of depression, shame, apathy, or grief that get absorbed by the developing child simply because he or she is there, not because it is necessarily the child's personal reaction to situations. We can absorb our mother's grief or our father's rage even if it was not about us or our behavior. Parents, peers, schools, and workplaces all send messages to and about people that bear no relation to what is occurring within an individual or what he or she is doing. Children become *lived through* and their open bodies and minds are the forms that can carry the intents of their caregivers. In the absence of strong self-movements these mesages get taken on and the self becomes defined. In the absence of self-definition people seek such answers from others and further the possession experience.[4]

Possession is far from the truth of our own self-movements. There is usually no personal truth in these energies at all and the maxim "you cannot work with any energy except your own" refers especially to possession levels—and it does not matter whether the intrusions were given with the intention to help or control.

Possession structures have no formlessness at all. They are the most dead of all the energetic formations in the bodymind. They would be the equivalent, on the physical level, of scar tissue. Once formed by damage to tissue, scar tissue has no further ability to change itself. It remains isolated from the life of the physical system that surrounds it and rarely gets metabolized into the surround. Healthy tissue can grow up around it and compensations can be made for some of the movements that were once mediated by the old structure, but it has no way to blend with the surrounding muscular system. Possession structures come about by analogous damage to the self system. They occur because there has been no support for individual movement, or the system has been assaulted by outside forces. The individual could not respond to the assaults with an adequate response or participate choicefully in the reactions. These psychological scars are the feelings, intentions, and knowledge of others that have come into the system and replaced the self. They are energetic introjects that could not be integrated into the self because there was no support for making choices. The only thing one can do with possession structures is to identify them and let them go by creating one's own equivalent solution. As I will discuss later, these structures cannot be healed by the process of blending. Instead, the individual must feel the experience that lies under the possession, whether it be a wound, a void, a state of chaos, or another belief system. Like a healing in which scar tissue is broken up, there is always an in-between state of vulnerability in which the old formations are gone and the individual is working to create another structure to support self-movements.[5]

It is often difficult at first to distinguish between defenses, possessions, and identifications, as they are interwoven into the identity and serve the same purpose— to solidify the experience of self and provide an answer to the question. "Who am I?" As consciousness proceeds through self-exploration, however, they feel different. As health increases it becomes easier to know what is self and what is not. Questions like "Is this what I really believe or is this what I was told?" or "How do I want to express my feelings?" help to bring consciousness to our reactions and create choices. You can sometimes hear in a person's voice that what this person is saying about him- or herself has another person's energy and agenda mixed in with his or her own. Finding ones own voice is the antidote to possession.

Possessions are stagnant and dead, and once you can feel the life within yourself they become easier to identify. Defenses produce isolation and prevent connection and, once felt, can be changed with choice and the willingness to risk. Identifications limit self-expression and are habits of the mind that are never challenged unless one enters the field of psychospiritual work. All of these structures run extraordinarily deep in the psyche and many people find, with some chagrin, that much of their experience of self has been what others have said about them, and that much of their participation in certain life experiences has been based on these introjected beliefs.

Fantasy is another set of activities and self structures that often have little truth in them. Fantasy can originate in our needs and wishes and begin in a healthy way as a mock-up for a possible solution to a problem. What starts as a vision and a healthy exercise of imagination becomes isolated from contact and runs unchanged by any further connection to reality. When the contents and the expressions proceed no further in their development, the energy becomes stagnant and no longer reflects our truth.

Each of the above formations makes some contribution to the dark side of the individual.[6] Identifications become unhealthy when they are never challenged or brought into consciousness. The others—the structures of possession, defense, and fantasy—become dark when they support isolation. In the healing process, each of these structures gets touched by consciousness and changed in a different way.

There is a distinction between the dark side and the shadow. Unconscious (shadow) material in the individual is not always dark, but the dark side prefers the unconscious state, since bringing a structure into the light of consciousness always brings it a little closer to being impacted and changed. Also, there is a difference between the dark-side structures and the presence of evil. Like health, isolation and the will to harm lie on a continuum of functioning that embraces a range of energies. The term *evil* primarily gets applied to those unhealthy-side behaviors that serve the *sole purpose* of destruction of life with consciousness (i.e., *the intent* is to hurt and eliminate choice and change). At times, both defensive and possession structures can and do support the expression of evil if the individual is not making choices to care about or notice the impact of what is occurring. However, isolation, separation, and resistance to change do not make a person evil.

One very important distinction that we will focus on later is the difference between the dark-side structures of the self and the energies of the emotional wounds that often lie under such defenses. The feelings and experiences of emotional and physical wounding have movement and energy. Defensive structures are utilized to separate from these experiences and movements, and they become part of the dark side when they become chronic, stagnant, and prevent any further contact with the life of the painful experience. Healing means bringing together the structures of health and the aliveness of the wound. Healing requires touching the dark side so this can occur.

These terms, *dark-side*, *unhealthy-side*, and *evil*, are meant to represent forces within the person and not judgments about the individual. They are also somewhat relative. Identifications are not unhealthy from the point of view of personality theory, since in most schools of psychology these structures would consititue the self. In psychospiritual work, the structure of the self experience becomes much more formless and these identifications include structural formations that sometimes have little formlessness. They can be the masks that prevent further movement and prevent deeper explorations into the self. They also can become dark as they resist change and force away contact.

In psychospiritual work one is embracing a different standard of living than the culture at large. There is more accountability for one's impact on others and more attention paid to those aspects of the self that prevent connection. The capacity for formlessness becomes an important criterion for evaluating the health of a pattern of connection. An example of this is the levels of shame encountered when facing the dark sides of the self. Shame would rarely be named as a dark or unhealthy force when exposed for the first time in therapy. Instead, it would be regarded as a basic emotional response resulting from intrusions and judgments placed on the self. However, it could operate later in unhealthy ways if continually used to prevent connection to the underlying feelings of vulnerability or wounding. All emotions and reactions can function in unhealthy ways when further change is prevented by their expression. Any psychophysical structure can be held in isolation and thus function as part of the dark side of a person. An illness can be part of the dark side (for example, if it is held in denial or judgment or worsened to manipulate others), as can the body, any emotion, any ability, or any attitude. Hanging onto pain and suffering can at some point be damaging to further development. Relationships with others can be based on behaviors and feelings merging from the dark side of the individual. The inner child has a dark side as does the adult. When these psychophysiological patterns become *chronic* structures in the bodymind they become strong attractors for attention and judgment. They become more solid and less accessible to healing. Regarding illness or fatigue with hatred or contempt prevents further consciousness about what might be occurring, and stops healing.

Healing and psychospiritual growth involve moving structures out of the shadow and then out of the dark side. The first involves bringing consciousness, awareness, and acceptance to the structure; the second means bringing the process through the remainder of the Formula for Change—taking responsibility, allowing release and the emergence of new answers, then creating new behaviors of connection.

The memories of our past that are held in shadow can function either as a foundation for future choices based on what we have learned, or as a ceiling that limits our future development. What we have experienced in the past is the wisdom that we use for our future—unless we do not have access to these learnings consciously and they unconsciously serve as blocks to more connection to the world. To remove the dominance of the past requires that it become conscious, that it come out of shadow and be blended with current knowledge. Then, the past can be the foundation of our knowledge.

Every individual who chooses to commit to psychospiritual work faces these internal structures. They can be perpetrators of harm to others or form the basis of self-destructive behaviors. They can be avoidant, depressive, passive, hostile, narcissistic, addictive, suicidal, or homicidal. The content varies but they share the quality of rejecting life and preferring not to be confronted or touched. They can be linked to the most evil of energies or the mildest of self-deprecation. They can be part of the most wounded of inner child structures or the most elegant of social presentations. They can have their origins in the most recent painful event or the deepest karmic pattern. As consciousness develops, the dark side continuously manifests itself as the strong magnetic pull of unconscious states of being that pervade our everyday life—the so-called "waking sleep" of the culture at large (Tart, 1994). The struggle for consciousness is exactly that—a struggle against the weight and solidity of dark side structures within the self that choose to protect, defend, and isolate instead of connect.

Dark-side or unhealthy-side structures provide the most resistance to change. **They have the least amount of formlessness in them**; prefer the most secrecy; contain the most judgment; are mostly organized around protection, possession, or control; and are often networked with the most painful and negative emotional states. The confrontation of these structures is the hardest part of psychospiritual work. The disintegration of these structures creates the greatest feelings of loss and grief since they have the least amount of formlessness and capacity to change. The disorganization of defensive structures in the personality (e.g., the false self, the mask, the adapted child) can be a long and difficult process since the physical part of the process (e.g., the breakdown of tension systems in the body and the healing of the cellular energy fields) can lead to many physical symptoms, vulnerability to injury or illness, or experiences of physical brokenness.

As I said earlier, many of the dark-side self structures were not initially created out of any evil intent or need or desire to hurt others, but rather out of the pain and helplessness of the child and his or her inability to solve the crisis. These structures become dark and unhealthy when they have been in shadow for years and have not altered their form or brought it into present time reality. When these patterns surface in the context of therapy or other transformational experiences, they have a side that, out of the pain, can and often does hurt others.[7]

The healing process that is associated with the dark side has a very broad range in psychospiritual work. The blending of good and evil or health and unhealth can be a process that ranges from a knowledge of self-limiting belief systems to karmic struggles with evil. People can get overwhelmed and hurt during in-depth psychospiritual work. The states associated with these patterns can surface and become dominant. Depression, despair, bitterness and rage, arrogance, and physical illness can take their toll. Facing our dark side represents one of the most difficult of spiritual tasks.

Health has to be constantly chosen and created, and is necessary to make certain kinds of spiritual connections. It is easy to stop along the way at "healthy enough" way stations when life is functioning well. It is both necessary and healing to do so. Usually only challenges from teachers or new life problems kick the student into more confrontation with unhealth. Since spiritual work requires the ability of the psyche to explore more form-less connections, it is mostly in these pursuits that touching the dark side occurs. Pursue health, strengthen connections, work with the lack of connection, reach out for further connection. The equation spirals outward.

Interactions with other healthy living systems also challenge our abilities to change and connect. Marriage, having children, connecting to nature, and working together are all invitations to create life with others. Doing therapy/healing work or working with certain spiritual processes requires using the healthiest and most fluid parts of the self to track the process and assist the client/student in finding his or her health. All of these situations require that the emotions be able to move and that the body be able to tolerate the feelings that occur with contact. Chronic tensions in the body, limiting belief systems, possession levels, and fantasy all limit connection sooner or later.

The actual amount of contact/change that takes place in connections depends on who is involved, but being open to the possibility of change also means that the contact process includes taking the needs and strengths of the other person into account and letting him or her make a connection with your needs and strengths. The other feels seen and you feel seen. This does not imply agreement, only consciousness; that is, I do not have to agree with or like what I see, only be able to contact it without judgment. This experience is an important one in therapeutic change and in all forms of interactions in which there is mediation, negotiation, compromise, and sharing. The structure or behavior patterns are brought into consciousness in an atmosphere of being seen without judgment.

The opposite of these healthy connections are interactions of control, manipulation, usury, or destruction, where one party is shielded against impact and the other is vulnerable. In interactions like these, in which one or both parties have no interest in healthy contact, there are always barriers to seeing/feeling the pain or need of the other person. If you do feel the other's pain, you will be altered by the experience.[8] We also have strong barriers to allowing weaknesses and pain to be seen by the other party. Most of our interactions fall somewhere in between these extremes, where I am willing to let you see some of me, willing to be impacted by some of your energies, and I am defended against the rest. The amount of change that can take place in our interaction depends on how much opening there is in these areas.

As we will see later, making connection with parts of the self involves the same process as making connection with others. All structures involved in the connection must first be seen (contacted) to be able to change. So in order to change unhealthy parts of myself, I must first bring them to consciousness and make a contact. Being willing to bring out the dark side of the self and regarding it with acceptance is the first step in altering its structures.

Chapter 5

Creative Disorganization

Health is the ability to sustain periods of both
chaos and order, stability and disorganization,
and make choices in the transitions.

In Chapter 3, I presented a model for the change process that included a phase called **release** in which there was a disintegration or destruction of some old ways of being and behaving. This disorganization allowed a change in the way the individual **received answers**, and allowed the individual to begin reaching more deeply inward or outward for sources of knowledge. If the first two phases of the change cycle (acceptance and responsibility) involve a change in attitude toward a problem and a change in orientation toward the problem, the release phase involves the beginning of significant shifts in the psychological, emotional, and physical structures of the individual. Acceptance and responsibility are phases in which the problem is brought *closer to* the self. The release phase is a turning point in the change process. It is the phase in which responses *out to the world* are beginning to occur. The initial response is one of letting go of the old solutions and structures. This disorganizing phase has to occur in order for more formlessness to be present. In fact, the release phase in the change process is often the most painful part of the struggle to allow formlessness to be present in the body and mind.

In psychospiritual work as well as in healing, the release phase and the receiving of new answers are identical processes. Thus release is also described as *the receiving of an answer*. When self-regulation and control are suspended during a disorganizing experience, the processes of self-(re)organization can occur. **Allowing life to touch you will create a release of the old answers and feeling states, and the release of old patterns allows new life to emerge.**

The experience of disorganization has been discussed a number of ways in the literature of change. It has been called **endings** (Keleman, 1979) when it takes place as part of a larger change process; **the dis-identification process** (Assagioli, 1971) when it involves changes in consciousness within a psychospiritual disclipline; or just **positive disintegration** when it results in a healthier integration at a later stage. All of these terms refer to the premise that some form of disintegration, letting go, or surrender of an old "answer" has to occur for change to happen, both in the structures of the psyche and in behavior. In this essay, I have called this process **creative disorganization.** The word *disorganization* refers to the aspect of the process in which old answers/forms/identities are being destructured, and the term *creative* refers to the aspect of the process whereby newly emerging behaviors, thoughts, and choices blend with the old structures and change the nature of the system.

Chaos Theory and Change

I mentioned earlier in this essay that recent developments in biological science have given us a picture of how living systems work with regard to being organized and disorganized. All open or dynamic systems (also called dissipative structures) can be perturbed by outside interventions of any magnitude and suddenly manifest states of chaos; that is, it is not possible to predict when and to what state of organization a system will proceed when perturbed (Prigogine, 1984). These states of chaos are the analogs of psychological crises; that is, transitional states between more stable periods of functioning when disorganization of an existing structure has occurred and a more formless process is dominant. Chaos theory (and the model of functioning it represents) is being studied in a number of human biological systems, among them brain states, heart rate regulation, and the titration of certain brain chemicals. All of these physical sub systems appear to operate according to the principles of chaos theory; that is, there are periods of smooth flow, turbulent flow, and more chaotic disruption followed by a return to order (Gleick, 1987).

This model appears to be a good match for what occurs in the process of psychospiritual growth. Encounters with the internal structures of the psyche or external problems create periods of disorganization. In the midst of those periods, opportunities for new kinds of reorganization occur. If we can extrapolate from these models of open biological systems to construct a picture of how healthy self structures might operate, we have several guidelines from which to look at the role of disorganization in the healing process and in psychospiritual change.

• Periods of chaos appear in all dynamic systems, and they represent both a necessary part of the order of a system and an opportunity for reorganization.

• Moment-to-moment daily activity as well as longer periods of the life cycle are characterized by alternating periods of stability and order mixed with periods of chaos and instability.

• Disorganization is not bad or pathological—it is necessary for any system to change, reorganize, or evolve over time. Living systems can renew themselves in such a way as to maintain their integrity.

•Health includes movements between order and chaos—between stability and crisis. Learning to contain chaos (formlessness) and stabilize crises, rather than eliminate them, is the goal. Health is not a fixed, stable, resting state, but a state in which there is always some chaotic variability.

•Instability and change can be the base out of which creative patterns arise, including new solutions to problems, empathic connections with others, and new states of health not yet experienced. Change and continuous creation can be a way of maintaining order and strengthening identity;

•The goal of reorganizing work is to learn how to contain and contact the formless and chaotic state and support the individual in bringing order when needed.

Disorganizations

Disorganization is an aspect of change in any living structure that contains energetic processes, whether that process is physical growth, emotional expression, or spiritual transformation. The experience of disorganization means that something is going into the death cycle. Structures are transitioning and changing—either willingly surrendered or taken away. They can go with a whimper or a bang, gently or in great turmoil. In psychospiritual development and healing work, there are some fairly basic situations in which disintegration takes place. Following are some of the ways in which disorganizations and periods of formlessness occur in the growth process.

Being temporarily disorganized: This is the most common way in which formlessness shows up—not knowing what to do in a situation; being without guidance or information; losing connection with familiar landmarks or people; getting overwhelmed with feelings; becoming ill and finding the body limiting what you can do; having too many pressures on you and getting exhausted and overstimulated; having to respond to too many things at once; or experiencing a trauma in which some basic assumptions about life become shattered (see Janoff-Bulman, 1993). The coping systems get flooded with information and all the experiences cannot be processed. These disorganizations can be traumatically triggered when one has been exposed to destructive energies, or they can be the disorganizing part of a larger creative reorganization.

Bringing an experience to completion: Some of the more painful moments in the healing process can occur when consciousness is directed at moments in the past. There is often a release of feelings and emotional expression that was suppressed when the events first happened. The finishing of a traumatic experience, the grieving of a parent or love lost, or the expression of feelings around an event that we knew happened but never really felt much about are all opportunities for completion. The finishing of these experiences allows the insights and the feelings to come together along with a new frame on how to respond in the present. These can be powerful and temporarily disorganizing experiences because of the emotional components that will accompany traumatic material from the past.

Letting go of a false self: The outcome of a childhood experience of neglect, abuse, or conditional acceptance is often a low self-image, poor connection with personal needs and feelings, and a certain amount of distrust, anger, and fear. Defensive patterns that promote isolation and protect against harm get developed and form the outer shell of the personality. The defenses and shame that naturally come with being treated poorly also result in patterns of relating that do not work in adult relationships. These structures of possession and protection, when carried into adulthood, are often too fixed and reactive to be useful in problem solving. And when problems do not get solved, the levels of emotional pain, stress, and exhaustion become so great that the person falls apart. If these crises occur at times when support systems are not yet established and the person has no help in forming new responses, the resultant disorganization can go on indefinitely. This level of chaos is very difficult to endure since it was not chosen but is the result of exhaustion and shame inherent in never having problems resolved. If support systems are available, the individual has time to reorganize new behaviors.

Giving in to overwhelming feelings: Sometimes periods of struggle are followed by times of exhaustion and feelings of weakness, and the individual needs more support. What feels like "disorganization" occurs, in which one does not have much ability to be focused, to be purposive, to perform, or to meet the needs of others. Strong, functional people have a hard time with these feeling states and often feel very disorganized when they emerge. Learning to receive support can often restore the necessary energies and assist in reorganizing new coping skills.

Finding yourself at a dead end: Many people come in for therapy because they experience themselves as stuck. No crisis, no emergency—just no movement or pleasure in life. Examination of the stagnant state (such as depression, despair, or confusion) will result in it "disorganizing" into other feelings, beliefs, and attitudes that may have more movement in them, and more choice can then be brought into the process. After examining the problems for a while, some familiar situation occurs in which the persons defensive structure breaks loose and he or she has a rush of feeling and new perceptions about him- or herself and the people involved. Feelings of disorganization and formlessnes often follow these events, since the old ways of giving in or controlling no longer work and new solutions must be created.

Being chronically disorganized: There are some people whose childhood lacked support and the constancy of caring that provides the development of stable structures for connection. When impacted by the outside world, either in terms of demands for contact or a focused application of energy, the individual becomes overwhelmed with emotions or feelings of anxiety and must dissociate or withdraw. Such people feel constantly disorganized in that these iinterruptions always shift their attention and they are unable to control focus and provide internal constancy. Therapeutic support is almost always needed to change this way of being.

Something new is emerging: A period of disorganization might occur as a result of some new part of the self emerging—a set of needs, more assertiveness, a new ability like lucid dreaming, or a yearning for some spiritual development. The disorganization in this case involves trying to understand what is happening; trying to integrate the new experiences or sensations or feelings; or allowing some new part of the self into consciousness and letting go of certain structures that get in the way of self-expression (such as a fear of expansion, shame, or arrogance). These emerging experiences might involve psychic or spiritual states of being and be very unfamiliar at first and difficult to handle.

Taking the self apart: Most individuals pursuing psychospiritual development have some goal involving disidentification and the process of removing restrictions to deeper personal and spiritual experience. We want to stay open to spiritual experience and let go of the dead and stuck patterns in the bodymind. This kind of goal will produce a constant encounter with disorganization and reorganization of the self. It is not a process one is always in control of, and it takes a serious committment to "the work" to engage in this struggle. As the work continues one becomes more familiar with the dimensions of formlessness and experiences more of its vast topography—direct experiences of space, meditative

openness, touching the Oceans, deeper bodily experience, and more connection to the energetic aspects of life.
These experiences alternate with the struggle to remain
conscious in everyday life, to notice the habitual states
of mind and the ways in which we avoid contact with
our surround. This struggle becomes a part of the self
experience—noticing how we grasp and cling to mental
and emotional structures that prevent the experience of
formlessness and connection to a greater spiritual reality.

      As these scenarios suggest, there are many levels of
disorganization and many different ways in which
people face periods of loss. There is almost always grief
as the most enduring structures shift, especially when
our fondest beliefs about life shift and the relationships
based on those beliefs begin to change. We can lose a
friend, a thing, an ability, a bad habit, an idea of who we
were, or a connection to God. We can give them up willingly or have them taken away. All of these losses require us to process the emotions and face the experience
of non connection. **Disorganization means temporary
disconnection—a withdrawal from familiar and known
ways of connecting to self and others.**
      Change processes—especially the long-term ones
involved in psychospiritual development—involve a
constant encounter with the structures of the psyche.
Those familiar ways of thinking, sensing, feeling, behaving, and being can appear so immutable that only a few
are actually challenged until something unusual happens. Then consciousness opens and a new level of perception occurs and previously hidden patterns can be
seen more clearly for the first time. For example, "I never
knew how much shame governed my behavior;" "I see
now how angry I have been;" "I never thought I could
feel this free or this loving or this alive." As the witness
function develops, more and more structures become
uncovered and can be opened to new possibilities. In

healing work, disorganization occurs in the three major areas in which individuals confront the habitual structures that prevent movement, connection, and choice: in the mental life and thinking patterns of the mind, in the physical structure of the body, and in patterns of relationship. Although discussed separately here, all these areas are deeply interconnected in their functioning. It is more accurate to say that all psychophysical structures have physical, emotional, mental, and relational components. Which of them initially forms the basis for the exploration process is based on what comes to consciousness first or what seems to create the most disturbance.

Mental Structures

Allowing formlessness to enter the field of consciousness and begin to work is one of the major tools in changing the experience of the self. As we make more space in the field of mind by living with more questions and being open to different answers, we rely less on thinking patterns as a way of establishing identity. Mental states emerge that are characterized by a more open focus of attention, and one can begin to witness how ones mind works to create thought patterns. We literally begin to create our own reality by our mental activity. We begin to see many of the routine activities of mind as barriers to contact (such as fantasy, obsessive thinking, worry, or being lost in thought), and we challenge their necessity and their truth value. The "wall of words" (the use of words as a defense against the experience of space) can be penetrated and states of mind that do not include volitional or obsessive thinking can emerge and take their place as part of creative and spiritual life.

The mental experience that occurs when the usual habits and structures of thinking are changed can be felt as quite disorganizing. This experience can run the gamut from a gentle letting go of some belief or prior conception to an explosive bursting of one's personal identity and the sometimes crippling experience of complete loss of control. It can feel like changing one's mind; surrendering to a higher knowing; taking apart an outmoded belief system or way of being; or falling apart mentally, emotionally, and physically. It can take the psychological form of periods of confusion, chaos, sorrow, and loss; entry into the void; searching for something; incredible freedom of thought; a spiritual emergency[1]; or a mental illness. Spiritual growth entails challenging the usual schemas and belief systems of one's life, and the results can be as upsetting as when such belief systems are broken in trauma.

Formlessness facilitates the disorganization of fixed patterns of thought. This principle is behind the careful cultivation of the sense of space in all meditation traditions. In any spiritual practice, the interruption of habitual states of mind results in the emergence of material once held in shadow or not embraced because of its "irrational" quality. Examples of such material include memories of past experiences, awarenesses of patterns of behavior, emotionally charged imagery, archetypal imagery, psychic awarenesses, spiritual/transpersonal experiences, or energetic processes in the body. Throughout all of these emergent experiences and potential disorganization, the goal is to continue to make choices about how to express the emerging energies and integrate the new emerging information.

Body Structures

Sooner or later bodily experience becomes one of the most important aspects of psychospiritual growth. Although many spiritual experiences and energies first occur as mental experiences—that is, we see or hear the content first—they begin to impact the body as they are cultivated further. Spiritual experience, with its formlessness and different vibratory rates, challenges the fixed structures of both mind and body. The disorganization that occurs in the mind makes its way into body structures and shifts are required in the energetic patterns of the body. Health requires living in present time, and in the present-time moment all the systems of the bodymind are touched. These processes of disorganization will occur at all the levels of the bodymind, although the changes at the various levels of the person may occur at different times. Each channel of experience (Mindell, 1985) will show the disorganization differently and complete the emerging process differently. Sometimes there is a dream in which certain shifts in the psychic structure occur—certain things are completed or integrated—and only much later does the body let go of the emotions. A symptom, a tension, or a somatic reaction will occur. The physical aspect of the reaction is a measure of how deep changes must go to be completed and fully integrated, and how important an awareness of somatic reality is in the change process.

Consciousness can also go in the opposite direction. Illnesses and other body symptoms that require attention can deepen the experience of body and reveal belief systems and cognitive schemas that reflect isolation and withdrawal. Recovery from illness and surgery can be greatly influenced by other bodymind structures that are touched in those areas of the body trying to heal. For example, healing from surgery in the genital areas can be influenced by a history of sexual abuse. As earlier beliefs are changed, the energetics of the body shift and more healing occurs. Bodies are held in their fixed structural (characterological) patterns by our belief systems, by the presence of possession structures, and by longstanding habits of rigidity and participation in rituals. Participation in bodywork directly challenges the rigidities, while psychospiritual work challenges the belief systems that can hold the body in stasis.

The physical changes and the transformations of the body that occur with shifts in consciousness are often slowed down because of the potential emotional and physical pain involved. **The individual must consciously feel the body** in order for the process to proceed. Bodily feelings are more difficult to experience and are very real—they are some of the most dense and slowest moving parts of the healing process. The solidity of the body contributes to the seductive quality of pain and suffering, and makes it difficult to surrender the psychological attachment to the body. Aspects of our personal identity that are attached to specific patterns of somatic experience (e.g., the body image) do not change easily. It is frightening to have a different bodily experience. Many of the bodily changes that accompany disorganization feel unfamiliar and trigger anxiety.

The physical disintegration of an unhealthy self structure can cause an illness process to surface, highlight weakness in body functions or parts, facilitate accident proneness, or manifest the many somatic changes that have to occur as the body becomes more conscious. Many illnesses and somatic symptom patterns represent emotional processes that are being somatized instead of processed consciously. Whether or not deep emotional pain must be experienced for changes in the bodymind to occur mostly depends on which of the bodymind structures are being disorganized and changed. It is not a matter of choice, but of timing, since in most bodies the emotions have already been woven into the networks and will be released as the structures are blended with consciousness. Learning to contain the process and reestablish order where chaos was present becomes one of the requirements for healing.

The shifting of the body's energy to hold more formlessness and to hold the connection to spiritual realities represents an enormous commitment to health. Many of the yogic and Kundalini traditions have the knowledge base for these processes and emphasize how slowly the shifting of somatic structures must proceed to avoid injury and serious illness.

Relationship Patterns

Relationship patterns are another kind of structure that must change in order for growth to continue. Changing friendship and partnering contracts is very common as consciousness expands, as the individual begins to ask more of her or his relationships. The energetic exchanges must change to support more vitality. Giving and receiving become important in maintaining the vitality of the body and in focusing energy for creative projects.

The energy needed to maintain the healing process is increased when we allow others to touch us. In spiritual development, allowing touch by the world greatly enhances shifts in our self structures. Isolation prevents all such changes.

When relationship patterns disorganize, past messages, memories, and belief systems (often unconscious) are triggered. Like a divorce that opens up early recollections of parental love or abuse, each time relationships shift one has an opportunity to look at previous hidden assumptions and beliefs, and make changes to support better connections in all other relationships. Voids are touched in which missing information about how to relate is made conscious. Bringing formlessness into a relationship can be learned—practicing acceptance, taking responsibility for one's impact on the other, and being willing to change with the other can be done more consciously.

In spiritual development, the dimension of relationship becomes more and more important. Preserving relationship connections becomes more important than saving any particular individual self structure or behavior pattern. The connection to spiritual reality becomes more important than preserving a particular individual identity.

The Fear of Breakdown

Not allowing any disorganization or disruption to occur during periods in which there are important problems to be solved is certainly understandable. Each threat of disruption also has attached to it some kind of judgment and belief system around what it means to surrender, give up, let down, feel weak, die, or go crazy. The spectre of losing control is not easy to handle. The culture at large views any form of mental or physical disruption as a sign of illness and pathology, and finding support for these experiences as potential growth experiences can sometimes be difficult. But there are serious consequences in attempting to control all of one's behavior and not allowing any disorganization. Since the emergence of formlessness is a necessary part of the overall functioning of any living system, the unwillingness or inability to consciously hold the experience can have consequences elsewhere in the bodymind.

> A friend of mine whose son was killed several years ago was sharing the experience of his grief and his recovery. He was talking about the formless nature of deep grief and the difficulty of accepting the helplessness, the loss, and the accompanying dysfunction. He talked about how each cycle, when it recurred, made him wonder whether any progress had been made at all, and how he had no control over the releases of feeling that would occur in places he could not control. He said that acceptance of the grief was what enabled his healing to occur—entering the state and letting the process proceed without hindrance.

There are several options on the route to structural change. Ideally one allows the emotional pain to surface, grieves the loss, faces the changes, and begins to work in the formless spaces and create new solutions. Less ideal are solutions in which repressive and/or defensive measures are strengthened, old forms are propped up, and change is prohibited. Less ideal yet are solutions in which the old forms are practiced so long and so hard that the system finally explodes in violence or implodes in illness with so much force that there is no basis on which to create a new structure. The latter reactions to impending disorganization may take several forms: physical illness, disorganization in one's mental functioning, or havoc wreaked on the people around one (see Flach, 1988). In any case, the energies of destruction will have their day—either in the optimal mode of facing formlessness, or in a reactive mode on some aspect of the bodymind. The phenomenon of disorganization itself includes the energies of destruction as a part of all creative acts. As all spiritual growth systems have emphasized, death is a part of the life process, and putting self structures into the death cycle is part of keeping the self alive.

If there is any guideline to determining the degree of disorganization that occurs, it is this: **The degree of experienced disorganization is proportional to the degree to which there is no formlessness in the structures involved.** That is, disorganization is much harder, more upsetting, more unfamiliar, and more disintegrative the longer the current "answers" or structures have been in place; the more they have been imbued with judgment (i.e., being right); the more they involve control or possession of others; and the more they were organized as a result of trauma. The less one can handle the states of formlessness, the more difficult disorganization is. If there was a lot of chaos in the environment of the child, then chaos is experienced when the defenses are disorganized. If the wounding was malicious and evil, then the self structures underlying the protections will be more shattered and broken. Chaos and voids, as experiences of formlessness, come from neglect and harm, and the accompanying disorganizations that occur during healing only reflect what occurred before. Sometimes we are able to let go of some structures easily and softly move to new behaviors. Other disorganizations reveal more of a trail of destruction.

As possession structures are identified, one has to face the formlessness and voids that the introjected answers once filled. If we have been told who we are, we must now choose who we are going to be, and then form appropriate behaviors. When defensive and protective structures dissolve, the truth emerges and painful feelings and experiences of wounding emerge. Fantasies, when surrendered, leave us with the original visions, and we must move and choose what we will create. Identifications automatically change when something new is created. As individuals make deeper connections with the life around them, they change who they are and the old selves become absorbed into the emergence of new energies. There is no need to attack the self to change. Simply beginning the process of creation will shift the existing structures.

The longer and more fixed the "answer" has been, the more difficult the experience of disorganization will be, the more loss will be felt, and the more disruption there will be in the process. When an individual is letting go of some belief, pattern of response, idea of who he or she is, relationship, or situation that has served as an answer for a long time, and **has not changed,** he or she is more likely to feel disorganized, confused, and lost. This is why healing the wounded child is painful and can take some time to work through. The reverse is also true. Structures that have retained their questions—their sense of openness and opportunity to move and change with continued contact—can be altered without much sense of disintegration. **Change is possible without the experience of loss.**

Early phases of the commitment to personal change are often the most difficult. The structures being altered have been around for a long time, are often defensive or protective in their function, are associated with strong emotional reactions, have strong personal meaning, and only are let go of with a lot of pain. Changing the structures of the dark side can be very painful—but if they are not changed they become self-destructive. Opposing disorganization means opposing life. Forms of behavior that no longer support life must be literally destructured(put to death). **If you cannot put a lie into the death cycle, it will turn and become a murderer.** If the wounded child does not grow up and blend his or her needs and expressions into an adult mode of functioning, that wounded child will harm the adult's creative expressions. Old ways of being that persist in spite of changing needs eventually harm those who hold the structure intact. This goes for individual self structures as well as group mentalities in cultures.

Although we have talked mostly about unhealthy structures and the difficulty of letting them go, similar considerations apply for strong bonds of attachment that have been operating for long periods of time. The sense of loss and pain that occurs when a parent, old friend, or spouse leaves or dies can be related to how much this person has become a part of your identity and how important his or her way of being has been to your stability. If the relationship had not shifted much over the years—even if the interactions were pleasureable, stable, and part of ongoing life—the tearing and loss experience often reflects the lack of formlessness in the structure. I have known people who have been able to truly celebrate the transitioning of a loved one while also experiencing the loss. This ability accompanied a connection during the relationship that celebrated change in the other person.

It is important to remember that the goal of healing is not to only produce releases of the old ways of being, but to provide a context in which new answers can emerge. You can never know what will emerge once the change process begins. It is not a controllable process. **What is known is that the seed of the emerging answer lies somewhere in the depth of the old structures.** States of health emerge out of the formlessness and chaos that accompany disorganization. New life emerges as old patterns are allowed to die. Whether those new answers take the form of new ways to look at old experiences, new movements of the body, spontaneous creative ideas, or more clarity about one's purpose and goals, will depend on what questions are asked and what the individual needs. What is needed most often is an ability to "surf" or "ride the waves" of these disorganizing experiences while the new answers emerge and can be examined in consciousness. Sometimes this can only be done in the context of therapeutic work[2].

Surrender

Another kind of creative disorganization that occurs as a part of psychospiritual work is **surrender.** In surrender, a person willingly embraces the idea of letting go of attachments for a higher purpose—namely to cultivate experiences of formlessness as part of the process and to receive answers from new sources within and without the self. One must learn how to let go of control, to flow, to accept what comes one's way. We cultivate the ability to do this—to surrender to our feelings if they are blocked in their expression; to surrender an exclusive committment to our personal needs to include the needs of others; to surrender a strictly personal agenda to include some higher level of order or purpose (e.g., "God's will"). Forgiveness of others is a form of surrender. All of these surrenderings require that some existing beliefs or agendas be dismantled and that we open to questions. What am I really feeling? What can I change here? What is God's will for my life? Even surrender, which often is entered willingly, can be painful, disruptive, and resisted at every turn.

The process of learning to surrender, however, gives us a look at how disorganization can occur with choice and what has to happen to actually let go of an old structure in the bodymind. Usually, changes in the self structures fall into the catagory of "don't fix it until it's broken." We depend on outside forces to move us. Then we say, "I give up," and begin to let go. That scenario illustrates an important feature of structural change—**that is, something outside our existing range of consciousness has to impact us and bring a problem to our attention.** This intrusion could be an upwelling of the inner life or a relationship problem or a body problem or an outside world problem or all four. Another could be a teacher or therapist naming certain behaviors that are self-destructive or naming beliefs that are limiting us. Now we are in a crisis—a transition. This feature of the change process is not a criticism of how people operate, but reflects one of its basic principles—**we change through connection**—through letting the outside world impact us.

From a growth perspective, we have to try to respond to these interruptions of our patterns in a way that enhances our life and consciousness—to move toward the experience and accept and embrace it. In doing so we have to examine the nature of our reaction (the impact it is having on us and others) and make some choices about how to respond. Often, we discover how limited our previous responses have been and how healthy (or unhealthy) these responses are. We also see what we can change. Almost always, we need more information. We are, then, in the question again. In bringing consciousness to the old pattern—in examining the old structure to see its fitness for the new problem—we have brought formlessness into the equation and have begun to change the form. We have started to activate creative processes in ourselves that will move us toward new solutions. Bringing consciousness and choice to a behavioral pattern opens the possiblity for change and makes it more permeable. Examining the choices we made, feeling the feelings involved, and naming the belief systems that make up the structure already makes it different and is altering its form. This illustrates another general guideline in working with disorganization. **Allowing the presence of formlessness and creating new structures or solutions greatly facilitates the disorganization and weakening of old structures.**

An example of this might be the process of healing depression, especially those depressions of a psychogenic origin (the so-called productive depressions). Many individuals encounter these states when they begin to actively pursue more aliveness—when they seek a deeper connection to themselves or others and discover there is a layer of despair and hopelessness that prevents movement toward others and generation of more energy. Going deeper into the experience results in its disorganization into different feelings (often sadness and anger), belief systems (negative self beliefs), and ego states (being lost and alone), and these in turn get to be worked with consciously. Different choices can now be made in situations that previously would have resulted in giving up, not connecting, or dissociating from feelings. In this process, one is destructuring many levels of structure—beliefs about the self (the negative self-image), stances of collapse and immobilization, and certain historical states of consciousness that contained little witness. The support to breathe, move, and express feelings differently; the mourning of what was lost; and the attachment to new sources of nourishment bring the old "depressive" structures to an end.

This guideline, that **surrender is accomplished best**

with the creation of new structures with more formlessness present, is why it is so difficult to just "let go" of old patterns by themselves. It seems as though all existing structures in the bodymind, once established, have a cohesion that originally supported survival, and now resist disorganization. There has to be a very good reason to change even small schemas and assumptions about how things operate. That reason is often that something new has been created and the old structure is no longer relevant. **The creation of new life is the best way to put something into the death cycle.** This balance allows the death cycle to proceed without becoming murderous to the individual. Examples of this might be deepening a relationship with someone while experiencing loss in another arena, building something physical like a garden while grieving, or helping others in order to bring life into your own death cycle.

People can get stuck in the change cycle in the beginning stages of letting go of an old pattern. As the feelings of pain emerge along with the experience of voids or wounds, the new structures are not yet strong enough to carry the day. The new self structures seem weak and incomplete while the familiar defenses or old ways of being seem more safe. An oscillation occurs between the painful experiences of the past and the new responses that are being established in the present. It is on this interface that the seduction of pain and the inertia of unconsciousness seem so strong. New choices and actions will help let the old structures go, but they have to be supported and formed in the present and in the question.

Surrender is, at its heart, a process of blending. It is the experience of moving into an old way of being or a new answer with more choice and consciousness. It is not the loss or rejection of self in favor of someone else's answers. It is the blending of self-participation (sometimes, one's own need for control) with other sources of wisdom, information, or directives that you have allowed to impact you and that you have chosen to work with consciously. In therapeutic healing, surrender is best accomplished in stages while healthy parts of the self are being strengthened to do the work of containing the feelings and choosing new ways of being. States of disorganization or chaos (i.e., entering into states of being in which connection with others or choice is not possible) are sometimes unavoidable, but often are not helpful to the healing process.

Not all bodymind structures just dissolve and leave us with a clean slate. Disorganization means that new pathways for energy are being created and that old ones have lost their charge. The movement of that energetic charge from one network to another represents the emotional experience of disorganization, not necessarily the total removal of old ways of being or memories of trauma. Finding health means that new structural forms become more dominant—sometimes just leaving the old ones inactive, and other times actually changing their structure.

Encountering the many states of consciousness involved in change and personal growth is one of the most challenging aspects of allowing it to happen. The varied states of consciousness associated with the release phase of change will almost always involve the experience of surrender or letting go; some encounter with the experience of death; and some contact with chaos, emptiness, voids, or formlessness. Yet if support is present, new levels of functioning, creative thinking, new energies in the body, and a larger sense of self emerge at the same time. It is an incredible opportunity to embrace something of a larger world, both inside and outside of the self.

Chapter 6

Voids, Chaos, and Formlessness

A void is the absence of self movement—the experience of touching parts of the self that are not capable of connecting to the world.

In Chapter 2, the many faces of formlessness were discussed. The experiences that make up these transitional states vary widely. On one end of the continuum are experiences in which the individual is in reaction to the loss of connectedness to familiar objects. On the other end are situations in which there is a willing surrender into states relatively free from the constraints of limited self-definition and a connection to higher levels of order in the universe. Spiritual experience and ego transcendence are often described as the ability to connect to these higher levels of order and have them be resonant with the self. In one's work to achieve these states, there are many times when formlessness is touched and the experience is not so life affirming or ecstatic. Touching our voids and the chaotic parts of ourselves are two examples of such times.

The Experience of Voids

Touching one's voids goes to the very heart of psychospiritual work. In essence, all personal and spiritual work serves to move the individual toward completion—by supporting the completion of emotional responses around early trauma; by completing the development of mature behavioral systems that were aborted or never taught in childhood; by fostering the development of abilities that make us more completely human (such as intuitive/psychic development); or by facilitating connection to spiritual truths and a deeper connection to God. Gaining an increased feeling of completeness in any one of these areas inevitably creates joy and satisfaction and adds immeasurably to the quality of life. Two questions that constantly arise in this process are "Where am I not able to connect?" and "What is missing in my life / Is this all there is?"

These are, of course, the same question. **Where we are complete (live in our own truth), we can connect to others without losing our essential identity. Where we are incomplete and have voids we are not able to connect, since we are not operating with choice and we are unable to change (i.e., move, receive, blend).**

As a way of looking at this void phenomenon more closely, following is a partial list of some common therapeutic experiences in which people directly face formlessness in some more difficult ways.

Not knowing how to do something to get a particular need met—for example, not knowing how to ask questions that facilitate problem solving, or how to negotiate with someone, or how to tell what you are feeling.

Therapy always manages to highlight what we were not taught or have not practiced, especially as an individual begins to look seriously at his or her life and wants to begin to solve problems and create more. This goal-directedness invariably involves the discovery of both strengths and weaknesses and acknowledgment that our experience is limited in certain areas. The feeling of not knowing how to do something can be experienced as a void.

A lack of any definite sense of self, due either to a muted or anesthetized sense of the body, or an inability to make intimate connections to others in which they can make an impact on you or can receive love from you; having a strong psychological investment in a false self or a role.

Certain areas of emotional development (or the lack of it) get emphasized in personal growth work—the ability to feel safe, to have a fulfilling sexual life, to create physical and emotional vitality, and to intimately connect to others. Touching any one of these areas can lead to an experience of a void as it opens up into consciousness. Most people have only partial development in these areas, and what is missing comes into conscious awareness accompanied by a sense of loss or confusion. Many of these kinds of void experiences result from childhood deprivation or neglect. A feeling of personal emptiness comes from the inability to connect to others or to structures within the self that allow feelings and energy to move. The ability to feel alive and full is absent. When one becomes conscious of having a false or monodimensional identity, one often feels a sense of emptiness or void as the false-self structure is no longer fully identified with. This is the feeling of emptiness that often accompanies the narcissistic personality defense (Singer, 1977).

The lack of an ability to express and work with particular feelings (such as anger or rage, deep longing and needs for contact, fear or terror, feelings of helplessness or victimization, or sexual expression). Miss-

ing are self structures that allow the expression and experience of the feelings such that more choice can be
brought into the process and the feelings can be owned
as part of the self.

While in therapy most individuals face one or more
of these emotional expressions that at first may appear
to be nonexistent and then may later emerge as overwhelming threats to their present identity. Creating
healthy structures for the expression of feelings is a part
of therapeutic work. When these structures do not exist, the emergence of the feelings is threatening and will
be pushed underground, creating a void in the
individual's ability to connect to others. Instead of feeling angry or afraid or in need and still staying connected,
the individual will fly off into a rage, or dissociate, or
deny feelings—all of which are voids or "holes" in the
connection with others. Sometimes the inability to contain or process a feeling will result in the individual dropping into a "deep hole" in which he or she cannot name
the feeling, but instead feels helpless, immobilized, or
collapsed. These psychic spaces feel terrible and can
dominate the individual's consciousness. They are described as private hells, bottomless pits, ruts, dark
abysses, and so forth. They are often aspects of self structures or networks that have occurred as a result of trauma
or neglect and the person is reexperiencing the helplessness. These experiences can be the basis of the feeling of
internal chaos. The behavior accompanying these feeling states is erratic and usually noncontactful. These patterns are formed when a child is raised in a chaotic emotional environment.

**Being dominated by one's dark side with no
healthy structures to provide strength or nourishment
to fight the negativity. For example, having low self-
esteem, an inablilty to touch anything positive about
the self, and being overwhelmed with depression or
resignation or despair.**

Certain kinds of voids reflect areas of the psyche that are dominated by unhealthy belief systems and behaviors. In addition to not having a healthy structure to create connection, the individual has negative beliefs about him- or herself, negative feelings and behaviors that reflect an unwillingness to connect to others, a preference for isolation, and a desire to hurt others. These patterns become evident as these structures become conscious. Such awarenesses add another level of difficulty of working with voids, since most individuals, once aware of these unhealthy patterns, want to let go of them as soon as possible—often before there are enough new behaviors in place to sustain health.

Another source of void experiences comes with touching abilities that have been lost since childhood. When they begin to be claimed in adulthood they are often incompletely developed and seem formless compared to one's strengths.

An inability to "struggle" with life's problems—that is, to problem-solve and move forward with solutions.

Solving problems is a complex process that requires much self-knowledge. It means being able to move through the steps of the Formula for Change and tolerate the periods of formlessness without too much pain and distress. Without that self-knowledge (for example, with voids in the self structure) this ability is reduced.

A lack of development of certain psychic and spiritual abilities. Having no sense of one's psychic abilities or being a psychic person with no control over the experience. Not knowing how to express or encourage connection to God or feel connected to an order larger than the self.

The journey of spiritual development begins with the experience of voids. What we do not know, what we have lost, and what we cannot access is often the motivation for pursuing the spiritual life. One becomes conscious of the under-development of certain intuitive/psychic structures when one begins psychospiritual work and tries to learn the skills. Once one is exposed to the territory and possibilities for these abilities, it can be frustrating to experience how slowly they develop and how much they depend on ones emotional development as well. Other examples of these void experiences include certain spiritual challenges like the Dark Night of the Soul, where once familiar connections to a spiritual reality become broken and other kinds of spiritual voids are experienced.

Common to all of the above examples is the general principle that voids occur when there are self structures (couplings with the world) that are absent or not well formed, making connection difficult, or when the dark side of the individual is dominant and the existing structures resist consciousness and wish to stay unchanged, unimpacted, and in control. Voids, then, occur when individuals have chosen isolation over contact, or when a structure that is coming into consciousness has little capacity to connect. **The term** *void* **refers to that lack of connection—the lack of any process of witness, of responsibility, or of the ability of the self to choicefully participate.**

As these lacks in structure or void experiences come into consciousness, they typically are not neutral experiences, nor are they always seen at first as processes in which voids are being touched. There is enormous pain in touching empty parts of the self; the experience is filled with memories of abuse, deprivation, loss, absent fathers and mothers, strong emotions, and the tragedy of having to hide the self away from an unsafe world. The memory of loss or the yearning for one's connection to God can be as painful as the loss of a parent's love. Not knowing what to do or how to solve certain problems can be embarrassing. Sometimes, it is hard to even know what questions to ask.

In earlier chapters in this essay, I mentioned some of the ways in which the experience of formlessness could occur—in having something meaningful taken away, in looking more deeply into the self, or in actually seeking a deeper connection to spiritual reality. These experiences are also capable of producing voidness or emptiness because **both the experience of formlessness and the experience of the void are all about seeking connection.** Voids usually come into consciousness because something more is sought and one has to assess the capacity for connection. So the question "What is missing in my life?" becomes "What part of me or the world am I not able to connect to in the present?" This question is the first movement out of the void. **Asking a question is the equivalent of bringing in a more healthy, alive experience of formlessness.**

The Structure of Voids

The examples mentioned above are void experiences that are commonly dealt with as part of personal healing. The individual was confronting something missing in the self that is now necessary to complete a connection either to some part of the self or to some other person(s) or energy. The void is revealed to be a lack of an internal structure (either a belief, or an emotional or behavioral action) and an inability to make and hold the connection desired. Voids occur because something has not been taught; something that once existed was hidden away and not used or developed; or actual damage was done to the person and parts of the bodymind were destroyed or broken. Voids occur as a part of development when some aspect of the individual is not addressed at all, when it is punished or negated, or when someone else's answers have been a part of one's psyche. There are voids in all of us and in every family system.

Our families only teach us a part of what it is to be fully human and at this point in society, our culture tries to ignore the rest. We have poor models for what it is to be a fully human being; and finding teachers who have the capacity to bond, to love, to work, and who have developed psychic and/or spiritual abilities is difficult. All of this means that certain aspects of the self remain missing and are not addressed or challenged.

When there is a void in the structure of the self, it is typically not an empty space. It has been said that nature abhors a vacuum, and that principle applies here as well. **Voids only refer to the fact that there is not a conscious structure of the self operating with choice and capable of change.** There are often other belief systems and behavior patterns that serve to "fill the space" and enable the individual to remain protected or do something else to avoid solving the problem. These are the "ego identifications" of the false self. Most often those belief systems have been accumulated in development, sometimes absorbed from the early family environment, sometimes concluded by the child as an attempt to figure out what happened. Most often they are not even conscious. For example, if there is a void around expressing and maintaining intimacy, beliefs that might fill it in are: "I do not deserve love," "No one cares," or "My love is toxic."

If there are voids in sexual expression, dysfunctional beliefs might include: "Sex is wrong or dangerous" or "You owe me this."

If there are voids in the ability to make contact, dysfunctional beliefs might include: "I cannot afford to be vulnerable," "I am better than you," or "I despair that I can ever be loved."

If there are voids in the expression of anger, dysfunctional beliefs might include: "I am too much for you" or "I want to hurt you and that is a bad feeling."

Voids are also manifest in many of our reactions when avoidance, withdrawal, or punishment is used:

•I am afraid, but cannot say so and react by pushing people away.

•I cannot name or feel my shame so I react with rage.

•I want the touch but cannot tolerate the pain that might emerge, so I disconnect.

•I cannot express my grief so I shut off my feelings and become depressed.

Voids reflect the fact that we have many beliefs, behaviors, thoughts, and emotional reactions that occur unchallenged, are only partially conscious, and have never been "fully owned" and chosen by us. These beliefs and reactions make up patterns in the personality that are felt to be "us." They are "ego-syntonic" and fully identified with until some outside situation challenges their functionality, their usefulness, or their truth. They cannot be changed until they become conscious and felt and questioned. They can be beliefs about the self, emotional reactions or feeling states, conclusions about the world or other people, physical reactions or response patterns, or images deep in the psyche. Their origins are multiple[1], but if not consciously chosen or embraced (accepted) they serve to feed the experience of a void in the self.

The well-known phenomenon of trying to "fill" a void has been attributed to many patterns of behavior—especially addictive behaviors. Addictions become ways of identifying with or latching onto external structures or internal experiences (such as substances, relationships, causes, roles, bodily excitement patterns, and so forth) so the emotional pain associated with the loss of self is modified or only partially experienced. The person is afraid of dropping into the painful void experience and feeling the emotions that have not been completely processed. The opposite can also happen—the individual can become compulsively involved in recreating the experience as a defense. (For example, keeping the life empty as a way of avoiding the feeling of emptiness, or practicing nonexistence in life as a way of not touching the early pain of no connection).

When formlessness is present in the form of voids, there usually are few questions, not many answers, and a strong need to flee back to any structure—even if it is addictive, or a distraction, or not especially healthy.

The basic characteristics of the behavior patterns that cover voids are: (a) They do not exist in present time— they do not serve as current healthy wishes of the individual but represent an aspect of earlier ego states of the child, and (b) The individual is victim to them—he or she does not have control of the response system and cannot choose much about their expression. The static nature of the energy in such structures makes them feel dead and without movement—thus feeling like an empty part of the self experience.

The bodymind is often filled with beliefs carried over from childhood (or even before), resulting in deadness in the body, absence of need satisfaction, and no opportunity to bring in choice. Some of these belief systems and action patterns might have even been true at one time (as were defensive systems that once worked and were relevant), but are now lies. They are fixed structures that cannot change and allow questions. As most experienced clients in therapy know, examination of these systems is difficult and requires that the feelings surrounding them and the feelings of emptiness be touched. Voids stay voids because they are not challenged and because it is uncomfortable to touch them.

From an energetic perspective, voids are seen and felt as dead zones in the body and in the energy field. They are sometimes recognized psychically as another person's energy—as happens when the child was defined by the parents or other people. The structures of the self appear to be a series of fixed, stereotyped structures that reflect only what the individual heard from others—nothing he or she created through personal choice. The self structure is a series of disparate voices from the past—inhibiting the expression of a person's healthy selves. The bodymind becomes only a set of beliefs never examined, feelings never felt, and movements never made. In psychic work, there is a principle that says "you cannot work with anyone's energy except your own"—you have to feel and make a choice about what you believe, what you feel, and how you want to act in a situation in order to fill a void. If you do not know, then bring in a question like "What do I feel" or "What can I change about this situation?" and you will bring in an alive experience of formlessness. That is the beginning of movement and change. The act of bringing in questions makes a dead zone into a fertile experience. Feeling the voids can then be the first act of creation, or as a friend said, "Voids are the cliff from which you begin flying." Winnecott's (1974) remark that "emptiness is a prerequisite for eagerness to gather in" is also a wonderful phrase describing movement toward the question.

There is a vulnerability to the formless state that occurs when the individual is between the void and the question. Questions at least mean that some commitment to healthy behavior has been made and there is some attempt to form healthy new systems of connection. In this period the challenge to the unhealthy energies seems to get stronger. Depressions never felt so overwhelming, resentments so strong, weakness so painful, or wounds so crippling. As the defenses begin to shift and the old answers are less useful to the individual, the resulting formlessness is a mixture of chaos, voids, and questions. This is a time when support is absolutely necessary to find the energetic connection to the healthy side. Voids, like chaos, cannot be negotiated in isolation since their basic structure reflects a lack of connection. But that is just what most people try to do out of old habits—walk through the void experience alone. To

reach out in a void is part of the new structural formation and is a necessary part of the healing.

The Experience of Chaos

Chaos occurs during periods of stress and also during the healing process, and appears similar to touching
a void. **Chaos refers to the inability of the person to
bring organization into a psychological or behavioral
structure in order to connect.** Chaos means that the
formlessness in the self system is larger than that of voids.
The healthy parts of the self cannot be utilized to contain the movements of the emotions, the thoughts, or the
expressions of the individual. It means that the person
cannot get organized or feel a sense of integrity or sustained connection to a part of the self or another person.
Sometimes, the sense of chaos comes from early experiences in which the capacity to bring order into the self
was never supported, and the individual was left with
feeling unable to connect to others or regulate bodymind
processes.

There are many reasons why a person might not be
able to sustain or contain an organized connection process. Most people have moments or short periods of
chaos in which they cannot "get organized" or focus or
connect. Anxiety, exhaustion, or any number of emotional states can flood the bodymind and interfere. External distractions that are chaotic can create that same
state in us—like exposure to a person in chaos or an environment in which there is no order. Powerful emotional work in therapy or certain mind altering techniques (including drugs) can interfere with an
individual's ability to get focused. Like most mental
abilities, the ability to focus one's attention (on the outer
or inner world), make choices, and self-regulate one's
behavior is a learned process. It is usually learned and

practiced within certain parameters of feeling states, and if emerging emotional states become too intense, the ability fails and there is a moment of disorganization and chaos.

There are some individuals for whom this chaotic experience has been a regular part of their self experience. Neglect or an absence of contact, an unstable parenting experience, and repeated childhood trauma are all possible sources of chaos that could prevent a stable sense of self from forming. Under these circumstances, the *organizing process* itself can become damaged and unstable, and the result is a poorly formed sense of self and a chaotic mental and emotional life.[2] Here is how one person described her experience with chaos:

> My ideal-self said that I should be totally organized—I should BE HERE NOW!—have things all figured out, know what to do and just do them. But when I touch these feelings, everything I've done gets erased. I can't even remember the person that does good positive things. I feel like I'm dancing as fast as I can—spinning my wheels. I get pulled into this big hole and I hate myself. Everything goes—my eating patterns, my exercise, my projects. I'm out of control—it controls me and I am helpless to help myself.

The experience of chaos is often maintained because the primitive and unordered emotional states of the neglected or abused child overwhelm the self's capacity to express the feelings functionally. The emotions are like wild horses running without direction and sabotaging attempts to order behavior and bring cohesion into the experience of self. A person can sometimes use external supports to bring in order—like a work setting, where there is lots of structure, or a close relationship with an organized person—but to dip into the experience of self becomes much more risky.

Experiences of chaos interfere with allowing healthy formlessness to be present. The emotional by-products of a feeling of chaos are so great that holding a question becomes almost impossible. Voids continue, are not solved, and the connection process remains extremely difficult. The more the organizing process itself has been damaged, the more support is needed to proceed to the experience of facing voids. The more voids are surrounded by unprocessed emotional pain, the more support is needed to complete those emotional processes and be able to "hold" a question and negotiate the experience of formlessness.

Chaos and Change

Formlessness, as chaos or voids or space or any of its forms, can be either a healthy or an unhealthy state. What matters is how it is negotiated by the individual, supported by those around her or him, and moved into a process in which more functional levels of organization can emerge. States of chaos can generate creative processes (a kind of gestation state) and contain the potential for organization. Self structures that resemble open dynamic systems have periods of chaos built into their functioning that can lead to higher levels of organization. These chaotic periods can last moments, hours, or days. They can coexist along with other ego states. What this means to the individual is that periods of chaos can be followed by experiences of greater self-knowledge, insight, awareness, clearer thinking, different perceptual frames on problems, and more adaptive thinking about issues. Many of these new organizations occur outside consciousness—in the preconscious mode of cognitive processing (Kris, 1953)—and move into consciousness in many different forms. Dreams, symbolic insights, new thinking about a problem, and different reactions to old triggers occur spontaneously after such reorganizations occur outside of awareness. The energy of chaos and formlessness has, in spiritual teachings, been referred to as the "fertile void," and this phenomenon is seen in everyday struggles with problems. The main ability needed is the willingness to reach out with questions and grapple with the emergence of new solutions. Healing often requires that such moments and periods be supported rather than immediately filled with someone else's answers or solutions.

There are many levels of voids in the bodymind, reflecting what we are capable of as humans in our development and reflecting all that it is possible to connect to in the universe. There is no finished product or end to completeness, since I can always add to myself by connecting more to the world. In all therapeutic work, there is a need to end the pains of childhood and past losses, begin releasing the emotions associated with those experiences, and bring choice into the beliefs formed by them. Becoming complete, then, is being able to live in the present.

It is not possible to change the past except in memory or fantasy. If one's history contains experiences of abuse and certain aspects of the self have been broken, these wounds cannot always be healed by known therapies. The healing task, therefore, is to seek completeness by building new structures of life experience that are healthy, satisfying, and joyful, and to seek present-time connections of strength and wellness. The voids are always there, as shadows of the past, and may always serve as containers of some feeling.

Stages of psychospiritual work in which the individual is functioning well and mostly living in the present involve making additional connections with formlessness and asking, "What do I need to connect to now? What would extend me and bring out aspects of myself that I have not yet seen?" New problems will come into the life space requiring that these questions be faced. It is a given that the battle with the dark side will continue andKarma will serve up new experiences.

There will always be problems to be solved and voids to be addressed. **The experience of voids here means that the individual is reaching to connect to a larger universe.** The increased consciousness that is achieved in personal growth will inevitably lead to touching places where one cannot connect. The individual begins to see more clearly the need to create more self structures to bridge the gaps and reach out to the world in new ways. Isolation is felt more acutely and voids are painful experiences. The self structures that once served as the bulwark of the personality are now experienced as patterns that maintain spiritual isolation.

For strong and highly functioning people, facing voids can be very painful. Such people do not know how to ask for help and often fight strenuously against the unknowing and vagueness that can accompany the process. Yet life will force the experience on anyone. Learning to connect to larger and larger orders of complexity is a necessary part of development.[3] To not do this is to stop developing. Spiritual reality is such a larger order, and examining spiritual questions always precipitates some kind of experience with voids and formlessness. As human beings we have deep structures in the bodymind that allow us to connect to our souls and the Godhead (i.e., we have bodies that can receive souls), but we often lack the knowledge or the training to do so.

In the next chapter, I would like to address the final aspect of the Formula for Change—the process of reorganization of self structures and the development of the healthy side.

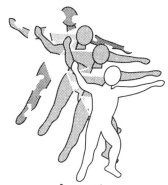

Chapter 7

Reorganization

The first container for the energy of chaos is a question.

The last two parts of the change process described in the Formula for Change in Chapter 3 are *Release* and *Change*. In the Release phase, old forms of behavior are allowed to disorganize so new answers can emerge. In Change, these new answers must be used to create new behaviors, new ways of thinking, and new bodymind structures that are healthier and contain more capacity for movement, choice, and connection. This is where people have to stretch, learn, risk, and create. They have to **do** the answer.

Thus far we have seen how one experience of formlessness—the ability to be in the question—begins to penetrate into the change process through the practice of acceptance, taking responsibility, and, if necessary, allowing the movements of disintegration to occur so new questions can be asked and new answers received. Then, new forms are allowed to emerge or are created that facilitate connection to a larger world. We are hardwired for such connections. We have bodies that can connect to the planet in ways few have developed; we have structures for mental abilities and for psychic and spiritual connections that go unused. These structures are created from and in formlessness. They come from the mystery within ourselves and mediate the connection to the mysteries outside ourselves.

Those who have observed the change process within themselves know the many ways in which bodymind structures can become reorganized. There are *spontaneous arisings* of new thoughts and feelings—a new perspective on things or a deeper sense of meaning about life that emerges as experiences are processed. These kinds of **self-organizing** miracles often occur during healing moments when new ways of thinking about or processing painful experiences emerge that shift the interpretation of the experience and leave the individual feeling more empowered, less ashamed, and less trapped by the past. The self-organizing process is often revealed in those transitional states in which control has been suspended or the bodymind has moved into an alternate state of more formlessness. People also find themselves *reaching for new meanings* or understandings in moments of need or when chaos is present—actively struggling to form a thought or a movement that is healthier and more adaptive to the problem. We can also *use existing knowledge*—trying out the truths of a healing text or a spiritual practice to see if they fit in our circumstance and can be embraced as a new way to be or look at things. Or we can, by trial and error, *attempt new movements*—working out of voids and formless places to form new ways of being that serve to better connect us to life. Reorganization is the creative process made physical and real—doing the answers that have emerged out of our process to see if they fit and serve us well.

In the next two chapters, I will describe some of the ways in which the creation of new structures of movement can enhance health. One is how we form new behaviors when touching voids or chaos; another is how bodymind healing can occur by blending present-time truths with the unhealthy-side structures; and a third is how the organization of new ways of being occurs through blending of polarities.

Organizing Form from Chaotic States

States of chaos in the bodymind, like all the experiences of formlessness, can vary enormously. They can range from temporary moments of feeling overwhelmed in the middle of a stressful day to the longer and more painful periods of feeling totally disorganized, unable to self-regulate, or make sustained contact with others. Chaotic states can be reflected in the attention mechanism (the ability to focus or concentrate); can show themselves in an inability to organize meaningful thought processes; or can penetrate into the body and be manifested in a runaway physiology that cannot achieve homeostasis, or in a hypercreative cell process like cancer. Like all states of formlessness, chaos is a normal aspect of development if it is contained within the boundaries of the creative process, and a destructive experience if it is not.

The psychotic, autistic, and schizoid mental disorders—all examples of serious illnesses—are conditions that arise when the individual's ability to organize contact has been damaged and has failed to recover (Hedges, 1994). The reasons for these failures are complex and multiple, but can occur because of a genetic pattern, nutritional deficits, toxic exposure, or failures in caregiving. The critical periods for such abilities to develop occur early in life and form the foundation for further personal development. The exposure to chaos can occur anytime, however, and is seen vividly and frequently in the life stories of children who have been raised in households where there is abuse (including substance abuse) and poverty. When a child is not contacted in a way that helps him or her reach out and participate in eye contact, loving emotional connection, or touching another person to exchange emotional nurturance, his or her ability to do those tasks can be damaged; such activities cannot be used later in life to get needs met, calm or nurture the individual, or facilitate healing. Contact can actually be painful and will be avoided because of the traumatic memories that might be touched. Since contact is the major way in which emotional states of distress, feeling overwhelmed, or trauma are stabilized and healed, the individual is without any way to organize new responses and create other ways of being in the world. It is difficult to self-regulate emotional states of distress even with an adequate history of contact. It is impossible to do so without it. **Bringing organization into states of chaos is first and foremost done with nurturing connection to another individual (or life form) not itself in chaos and able to contain the contactless (chaotic) experience.** Within the context of such connections, individual skills in self-regulation can be taught as the individual is able.

Similar principles hold for all levels of healing and touching the chaos within. All people have spaces in their self structures where they have experienced chaos and have not been able to organize a way to be in the midst of stress or trauma or a missing connection to another. Bringing order to these states is done in the context of connection as well. The loving touch of another person helps reorganize a connection to self when one is facing pain. The prayers of others can help to reorganize a spiritual connection when it seems broken. The ability to self-heal or self-regulate states of chaos is dependent on having a strong enough healthy side to connect to the chaos and blend with the experience. The key is the ability to participate in the remaking of the connection and to use the other person or state of consciousness as the foundation for reaching out.

Organizing Form from Voids

The touching of voids is a natural consequence of

psychospiritual work. As individuals reach for what is possible within themselves, they most assuredly will connect with what they cannot yet do. In healing work, the voids most often deal with the ability to make emotional connections to others and relate to the world in a participatory, noncontrolling, nonpossessive way. In spiritual work, the voids most often relate to the ablity to move out of the local, isolative experience of self and touch other dimensions of energy and movement in the universe.

One of the more difficult experiences in reorganizing new behaviors occurs when an individual is working from a bodymind structure that contains a number of voids—that is, there is a substantial amount of missing information about how to negotiate problems in life, and the self-identifications are based on defensive patterns, possession, or fantasy. If childhood neglect is the reason for void structures, these "experiences of omission" become the basis for pain and suffering as deep as any trauma. To not connect to a developing child in your care is to prevent that child from knowing who he or she is. The lack of contact prevents the formation of the self-movements necessary to form connections to the world. Instead of self-knowledge based on self-movements, the individual becomes dependent on the answers of others and on his or her own protective responses. Those possessed will seek possession until the process is uncovered. The outcome of neglect and possession is not an empty slate, but a behavioral foundation in which the structures contain both absent and dysfunctional information about connecting to the world. Neglect creates emotional structures that are primitive and reactive and are resistant to modification by present-time experience. The individual is unable to organize sustainable or satisfying connections to other people that would help him or her sustain his or her own health and creativity. Because there are fewer well-formed structures to work with, healing and self-organization require that the individual begin to form new behaviors and patterns of thinking from scratch. Since there are few inner structures to build on that are not defensive and dysfunctional, the healing is not so much a shift from one form to another, as it is a creation based on knowledge learned in the present—from present-time bodily experience, from mentors and teachers, from adaptive thoughts, and from created goals. Truly creating from formlessness in these instances means living with many questions, and learning health can be slow and frustrating at first. Highly conscious and intelligent people often get very discouraged at the difference between what they can imagine is possible in themselves and the construction of self structures to reach that reality.

When one challenges possessions and defenses and desires to let them go, one often feels emptiness. As one of the experiences of formlessness, emptiness often reflects neglect, and to work with it requires that the individual be able to feel the original emotions that accompanied the neglect. Emptiness means that there are no self-movements that are conscious, and to heal the state requires that the self-movements first felt (in response to the neglect back in childhood) be restored to consciousness and named—that is, brought into the question. Sadness over the loss, anger over the rejection, fear over the abandonment are all possibilities. Then, these emotions are brought into present time through the Formula for Change—acceptance, responsibility, release, and change.

As I mentioned earlier, the forming of a healthy self to work with states of disorganization, chaos, and voids means relying heavily at first on an "other."[1] Healthy connections with individuals who can themselves handle formlessness are essential to bringing stability into a system that cannot organize itself. **The function of such an external connection is to help highlight the healthy parts of the self that will eventually create sorganization and create a model for how to work with questions. It also assists in bringing the experience**

into present time. These connections also allow the individual to "dip into" the states of chaos or emptiness in order to take their measure and not be overwhelmed. There are many kinds of early experiences of neglect and trauma that cannot be brought into present-time awareness without the presence of a healing external force to invite the self out into connection. Certain kinds of trauma result in the individual losing his or her ability to *participate* in life—to reach out and ask for connection and caring. Without a loving invitation, the self-movement is stranded in voids and chaos.

It is easy to get lost in formlessness because models are missing for what would be the next step in creating new behaviors. The asking of questions provides the initial movement toward creating a structure that holds the possibility of more connection. **A question is the first container for the energy of chaos.**[2] What am I feeling? What do I need here? How can I help myself? What do I want? are forms that help stabilize the states that were created out of neglect or chaos. They allow witness to come into the experience and further allow the development of acceptance, the taking of responsibility, the release of pain, and the making of choices.

In individuals for whom there was neglect, possessions, and voids, the older reactive structures get left aside as new parts of the self get formed. The individual is encouraged not to rely on overly rigid or compulsive behaviors as solutions because they lack formlessness and are not in the question. They are much less easily altered to fit changing situations. Areas of health are constantly reinforced because they are the foundation for future connections to others. Working from voids requires connections in present time with sources of strength and knowledge. One must rely on sources of aliveness that come from bodywork, support of others, and psychospiritual teachings. Figure 3 describes an exercise in which the ability to receive support is explored with the help of a therapist. The individual cannot do it alone. Areas in the life that do work well are used as models for building the new behaviors. Order can be formed out of chaos and voids by developing patterns of behavior that feel good, give to the self, and assist in the connection to one's body, one's friends, and one's soul. Structures are built both from the outside in and from the inside out. Questions have to be held and many different answers tried. Filling in the missing information and facing the pain that contributed to the empty void spaces requires caring emotional support.

As the individual develops the ability to work with states of voids and/or chaos and begins to embrace formlessness as potentially creative instead of destructive, contact can serve to support and encourage formlessness instead of limit it. Many spiritual teachers assist their students by embracing them in an active field of consciousness that allows the body to increase its ability to move into formless states. Almaas describes one such procedure in his book *The Void* (Almaas, 1986). Jean Houston demonstrates exercises (Houston, 1994) in which she has her students experience everyday transactions at the personality, archetypal, and cosmic levels. Therapists as well are becoming aware of the need to support moments of temporary chaos and disorganization in their work with clients as they reach for new solutions to problems (Hager, 1992).

Working from Questions

Working from a question is the initial way in which some form can be brought into an experience of formlessness, voids, and chaos. As mentioned earlier, the most basic procedure is the **Formula for Change** itself:

1. **Acceptance** of the formlessness. Not fearing it as an experience but seeing it for what it is—a transitional

A Bioenergetic Process—Learning How to Receive

Individuals involved in the healing process need to increase their level of energy to do the necessary therapeutic work. To gain this energy, one must learn to trust and accept contact, receive support, ask for help, and nurture oneself. Neglect and trauma can close off openness for contact and leave the individual with no experience in receiving. Either there is a void (a "not knowing what to do") around connection, or an outright refusal to accept the touch because it might provoke the experience of trauma once again. The healer can offer a process that aids in the understanding of this dilemma and can give the client some experience in making forms for accepting connection and support. If the client is willing, place a hand on his or her back wherever he or she specifies and ask the client to notice how the contact is being received. Often, the person does not know how to receive the connection. The energetic contact, instead of being taken into the body, is diffused along the surface or not accepted at all. Make the suggestion that he or she might use the energy to warm the feet, stimulate the lungs to breathe more deeply, promote relaxation in the body, or just "be with" the connection. The energy usually begins to move and contact is accepted and deepens. The suggestion to create a form for the energetic movement makes the difference and allows the person to accept and participate (be responsible) in the contact. Receiving is dependent on the individual being able to participate in the process and bring some form to the energetic movement latent in this simple connection. The effects of this process can range from an new understanding of what receiving entails through strong emotional releases from connecting to past traumas or losses.

To broaden and deepen the experience of receiving, individuals can help create many more situations in which they participate in taking support or nurturance into the body by initially specifying what they want to use it for and what they want to happen. The goal of this exercise is to help one **move** along the continuum from having an unconscious reaction to touch, to **noticing** one's response, to **participating** in the experience, to **choosing** new actions that allow contact to occur. Bodies that can receive easily have a wide variety of forms to receive contact and are flexible about outcomes. This is not the case for someone learning all over again how to trust and accept connection. Simple steps can open the door once again.

Figure 3: An Exercise in Learning to Receive Support

space of changing connections. Acceptance means naming the formlessness, feeling it, knowing it, and separating out the emotional reactions from the sense of unknowing.

2. Taking **Responsibility** means entering the field of unknowing with questions asked "in cause." That is, questions asked, not from a victim position, but from a place of wanting to encounter the answer. Responsibility means that the individual is saying, "I wish to create an answer here that helps me connect"; "What is it that I can change here?"

3. The **Release** phase involves letting go of old answers that have not worked; identifying and releasing the feelings that were associated with the formations of the voids or chaos when the self was injured or ignored; processing the feelings involved in receiving the new answers; and cultivating those states that allow a connection to sources of self-knowledge. Release means coming more into present time and being able to hold the questions formed for a time, in spite of the anxiety of not knowing or the fears of not being right or stepping out in ones own behalf. Release is the powerful transition phase in which the chaos and the voids become fertile. The blocks to the new answers have been taken down and the creative process begins to move faster. Release questions involve asking "Is this something I can allow to happen without controlling everything?"; "Can I surrender my need to act immediately?"; and, "How best can I learn to trust my own answers?"

4. **Change** is the phase in which the new answers become more and more physical. This is the phase in which truths are spoken, written, and acted out in the present. Change is where the individual makes his or her sound in the world and begins to fill the void with his or her own forms. Visions and visualizations are moved into the physical and steps are taken to create new forms. Choice is strongly activated and new self structures are created. Questions in the change phase

include "Is it time to act on what I have seen, heard, or know?"; "Can I begin something without fully knowing the outcome?"; "What are the first steps to take to make this process physically alive?"

If formlessness has been allowed to enter the process from the beginning, it will stay alive in the creation of new self structures. Embracing formlessness means creating solutions that are fluid and not written in stone for all time; including others in the process for support and for exchange; and being open to being touched by what is created. Embracing formlessness means not controlling or possessing creations, but allowing outcomes to be governed by their impact on self and others.

Chapter 8

Healing and Blending

*The process that best describes the healing experience is
that of blending—when healthy aspects of the self
can be utilized to touch and impact the dark
side so new forms of thinking, feeling,
and acting emerge.*

Many times change occurs in people by the straightforward creation of new behaviors. We learn new things in situations in which there are no previous structures and new forms are created. We can imitate, experiment, generalize, and use all the mental mechanisms available to us to generate new structures to connect to the world. The process is exciting. If I learn energy healing, French, how to play golf, or work the computer, I expand my world and can form couplings with new things and people. New parts of myself are tapped and my universe becomes larger. These are the changes that can occur rapidly, especially if there are no competing systems to interfere. If confidence is high, concentration is focused, and conditions are supportive, amazing amounts of learning can occur in a short time and literally change the world we inhabit.

But there are also many situations in which we already have points of view—we already have established ways of being that are no longer effective, are underdeveloped, or even destructive. Past traumas have led to defensive patterns, confidence and self-worth are lacking, basic knowledge is missing or denied. In those circumstances, what we are seeking is a shift from one state to another. To make the new or different connections I want, I have to take the old structures into consideration since they still operate. Sometimes they operate in ways that are mostly unconscious. I only know that they interfere when I reach out or try something new, and I will have to contend with them if I wish to complete my connection. This means that some kind of **blending** process needs to occur within the self—some kind of meeting between the new and the old in which changes occur in both structures and I can get further along in expanding my world. The old structures have to become weaker and less dominant and the new ones stronger and more effective. Blending means that both the old and the new have to be brought into awareness—brought toward some kind of connection in present time. This means touching the limits of the old structures and their components—the thoughts, feelings, and relationship patterns involved. It also means letting those go while new patterns are being chosen. There is tension and conflict involved. Which one to invest in? Which pattern to follow? Health and non-health exist side by side—the way I want to be and the patterns I wish to change.

Blending

The process of blending information and energies is a fundamental part of many healing modalities and one of the most universal ways in which changes in the self experience occur. Following are some examples in which a blending process occurs in healing and psychospiritual work.

1. You have joined a support group consisting of

people that share your struggle. As you let yourself be-long to this group and receive their support, a sense of shame and isolation lifts and you can begin to share your experience in ways that help you find solutions. You can sense the difference in yourself as you open up more and accept their caring.

2. You are feeling down and someone you love gives you a hug. You let it in and your mood shifts. The self-deprecating feelings you were having about yourself get weaker, your sadness is expressed, and some good thoughts and feelings emerge. You are able to maintain those and the flavor of your day changes.

3. You are stuck on a problem and you decide to go for a walk. As your body begins to breathe and move so does your creativity. Some solutions begin to emerge and you are not so stuck.

4. You are in the midst of reexperiencing a traumatic memory and the therapist is present in a supportive and caring way. He or she helps you to construct another way of framing the events that happened, and supports you in expressing painful emotions. You accept his or her support and encouragement and complete processing a past injury.

5. You are recalling a past event that was very up-setting to you. You say to yourself that the event is over, that you are safe now, and you can bring yourself into the present. You breathe, feel your body, and stay with the experience. The fear subsides and you continue with your day. You "walked through" the experience with your own present-time knowledge and ability.

6. You are reacting with fear and anger to some-thing someone said and you decide to just experience the feeling instead of lashing out. You begin to feel your body sensations and the experience changes—the anger begins to dissolve and you get more calm. You can now connect to the person and talk.

7. You are doing a walking meditation and focus-ing on the sensations in your feet and legs. Your contact

with yourself deepens and you become highly aware of everything around and in you in a new way.

8. You have plunged into your own Dark Night experience. You continue to name it and walk through it by praying, reaching out for parts of yourself that give you strength, and trusting in those connections that you do feel in the present. You emerge from this experience with a renewed faith in yourself and a different level of connection to God and the world.

9. You have been seriously ill. In one of altered states that accompany the illness you have a spiritual opening. You communicate with loving beings of various kinds and experience a sense of awe, compassion, and a different sense of your purpose for being here on earth. This experience changes you dramatically and you emerge from it with renewed strength for healing and with a very different set of values about what your life is about. In some way, you have a different knowledge about what is meant by love, forgiveness, and your purpose.

In all these examples, there was a **blending** of different states of energy and consciousness. Either there was more witness, more consciousness or connection, or more nurturant healing energy brought into a state of being characterized by isolation, despair, past trauma, or destructive behaviors. These are the kinds of blendings that occur in healing and spiritual work—limits are transcended by the connection between the two kinds of energies or structures. The darker parts of the experience were touched and moved, and a shift occurred to another state. Health, in the form of acceptance, support, responsibility, or knowledge, touched the old structures and was in turn strengthened by the connection. The individual's healthy side now contains more of his or her past experience consciously and is a more complete structure itself. The movement of health into these old ways of being will also serve to highlight more of the dysfunction and create more release. In healing work, the process might continue until there is little charge left in the old experiences. The old structures are no longer energetically active but just a memory.

Blending is a universal process of connection. When it occurs, all participating structures change. It can occur within the self or between the self and the external world. It is involved in the healing experience as well as in psychospiritual growth. It is a strategy in the martial arts, in conflict resolution, in negotiation, in making partnerships, in vibrational medicine, in the use of imagery in healing, and in any of the alchemies of transformation. **Blending is a way of being touched and touching the world with a willingness to be changed by what you experience.** How much you are able to blend is limited by how much you are able to experience formlessness and be changed. The difference between the healing process and the fostering of spiritual experience is that in healing, one is touching structures that initially have very limited capacity for movement, and the timing, gentleness, and support requirements are higher. As the capacity for movement increases, more connections are possible with more fluid parts of the universe.

Healing

The process of emotional and psychological healing is one of the arenas in which these principles of change and reorganization can be applied. Healing is sought because there is a state of being that is in conflict with where the individual would like to be. Health is either envisioned or felt alongside the stagnation. In the healing process, the person is working with structures within the self toward the goal of processing painful experiences from the past, changing limiting and self-destructive belief systems about the self, or altering bodily reactions that produce pain and tension. To make healing successful, the individual must learn to reach out and receive support, develop his or her witness, learn skills to contain and tolerate the disorganization of defenses and face the wound, and learn to create an increasing level of health. This new health, in turn, is used to further the healing by supporting confrontation of larger chunks of the painful past, a body that needs attention, or unhealthy defensive structures. This is a spiral process, one step at a time, in which the boundaries between movement and stagnation become more and more permeable. Each time a healing process occurs, one's capacity for healing increases and one's abilities are expanded.

There are many forms and techniques by which healing can happen. Methods of healing most often fall into three categories:

1. Interventions that try to remove the offending tissues or processes and actually move into the body with some strong weapon that can destroy the toxic process or separate the remaining healthy part of the person from the illness. Methods like radiation treatment or chemotherapy attempt this, as do exorcisms, amputations, many types of surgeries, substances that create an avoidance of other substances, and so forth. These healing interventions literally "remove the offending hand" and allow the body to recover some degree of balance after it is no longer being impacted so strongly by uncontrollable destructive processes.

2. Methods that strengthen the healthy side of the individual by creating new thought patterns, movements, and/or supportive or vital connections.

3. Healing interventions that actually attempt to do a blending of health with the wound or illness process.

The most profound structural shifts in the transformation experience come when the disparate worlds of health and vitality come together with the structures of pain, despair, or isolation, and something entirely new is created.

To engage in the process of healing does not mean that something is "fixed," or even removed. Healing is a process by which the defenses and structures that wish to keep the wounds buried are gradually touched with consciousness, and the choice is made to release those defenses. Most often, it is the repression of the wound that causes the most suffering, leading to symptoms of distress, anguish, and an unchanging existence. Letting go of the defenses means that a death can occur, and out of that a new life process can begin. The life process lies in the wound itself, since it is the wound that carries the most truth in it, the most personal and essential information about our experiences and how they impacted us. Life cannot begin to happen again until the wound is touched. The ultimate goal of healing is not to remove the wound, but to remove its dominance and power over the life experience of the individual. The wound, together with the defenses, often determine so much of the contents of consciousness, that little else is created. Some wounds will never be healthy, but as they are included in the healthy side of the individual, they lose their power, and the knowledge of their limits and voids can become a strength. Choice over feeling and action is now possible where it was never possible before. The process is like adding more rooms to your house—some of the old rooms may still be dark, but you know where they are, and you stop trying to grow all your plants in them.

Change occurs by building on the life that has sprung from the wound. Without that new life, the solutions have a repetitive, stagnant quality, and resemble the patterns that occur when an individual keeps "doing the same thing" (like continuing to pursue addictive solutions instead of going through the healing process). If the individual cannot bring new solutions out of the wound, the healer has to help with questions and information, but only the individual struggling to heal can use that new information to bring the new life forward.

Sometimes it is difficult to keep the boundaries between healing methods that strengthen the healthy side and those that attempt to utilize a blending process. Increasing the movement of energy in the bodymind and providing vital and supportive contact will often touch other states of wounding that were not originally intended to be a part of the exercise. Even something as simple as a breathing and relaxation experience, an energy rebalancing, or an "opening your chakras" exercise can touch levels of wounding. If the situation is not organized around the possibility of some blending of other healthy inputs or support for the emotional pain, the possibility of retraumatization increases. What was intended as a healing or a strengthening exercise brings the indivdual in contact with painful experiences. For some kinds of trauma, it is unlikely that the individual, by him- or herself, can negotiate the experience without some cognitive, somatic, or relational support. Blending involves a conscious effort to create an environment in which there can be a corrective experience that touches the wound. These corrective experiences can come from within the healthy side of the individual as well as from other outside sources.

Successful blending, as it is applied to the healing process, requires at least three stages: (1) building strength and healthy structures in the bodymind; (2) bringing dark-side structures into consciousness; and (3) interweaving them in present time.

Building Health

The idea of building healthy structures for connection and choice is a familiar one in the personal growth field. It is the goal of every therapeutic modality, and is the promised outcome of most systems of spiritual work.

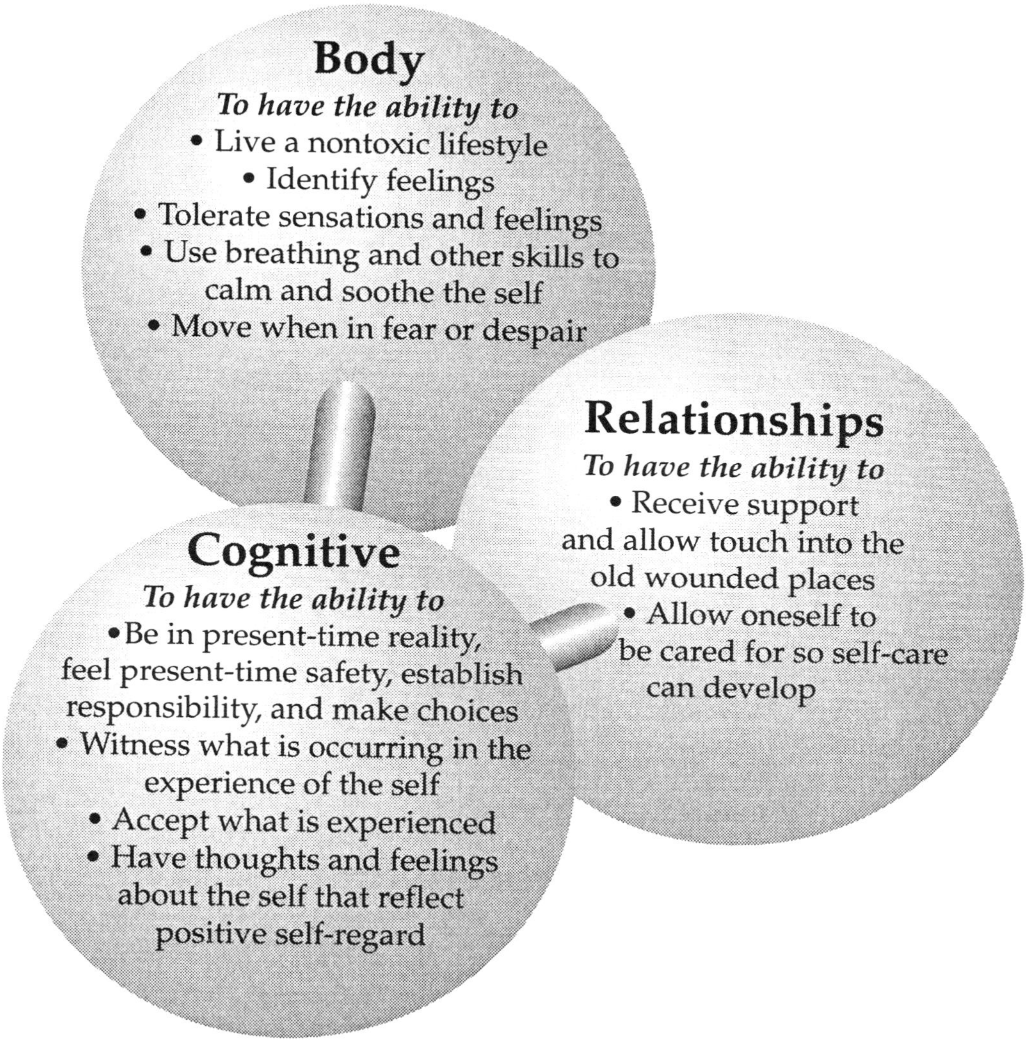

Body

To have the ability to
- Live a nontoxic lifestyle
- Identify feelings
- Tolerate sensations and feelings
- Use breathing and other skills to calm and soothe the self
- Move when in fear or despair

Relationships

To have the ability to
- Receive support and allow touch into the old wounded places
- Allow oneself to be cared for so self-care can develop

Cognitive

To have the ability to
- Be in present-time reality, feel present-time safety, establish responsibility, and make choices
- Witness what is occurring in the experience of the self
- Accept what is experienced
- Have thoughts and feelings about the self that reflect positive self-regard

Figure 4. Some Basic Bodymind Structures of Health Needed for Healing

All the fields of human potential work focus on this task and each field has its methods and disciplines to support the process. For healing from psychological and emotional trauma, there are some basic building blocks of health that have to be present. Since health is a constant choice, these skills have to be practiced and expanded on to increase the movement of the individual toward further growth. Figure 4 illustrates some basic abilities that are important in furthering healing—more fluid movements and emotional expression in the body, cognitions and beliefs that support change, and relationship patterns that provide support and nurturance. It helps enormously if there is some health being built in each of these areas, since emotional wounding often involves damage to all three of these levels.

There are also two important qualities of healthy structures of the bodymind that enhance healing. These aspects must be present either in the healer or in the healthy self structures of the individual seeking healing. One quality is the ability to be in present time and the other is multidimensionality.

All healing has to occur in present time. Essentially, our past as we recall it is some combination of memory and fantasy and our future is still only a fantasy. Neither the past nor the future has the aliveness to provide the energy for healing. So an individual working toward healing must have self structures that can be in present time—a conscious bodily experience of present-time sensations and movements that can be felt and tolerated; a set of perceptions, thoughts, and images that support an immediate experience of reality and being open to the question; and the ability to share a relationship dynamic that allows support and contact to occur in the moment. These are the structures that, when mobilized, allow the experience of wounding and pain to reemerge and be touched and changed. Only in the moment is there sufficient movement and aliveness to move the stagnation of the unhealthy side. Only in the moment can choices be exercised.

When we are living in present time we are **separate but connected** to our past. We have moved our past experience out of the shadow and are able to make choices about how we use the learning so it does not operate as a ceiling but as a foundation. Working with the unconscious allows us to have choice about our past experience and bring the knowledge into present time. Being in present time includes holding separate and disparate experiences in consciousness so some kind of blending can occur—so the phases of transformation as illustrated in the Formula for Change can proceed. Healing means bringing the past into the present instead of returning to the past and operating from that reality. If one cannot recall the past or work with what has happened earlier in life, it is possible that he or she does not feel their healthy side as strong enough to contain the earlier experiences. Either the past is viewed as more powerful, more or less desireable than the present-time life experience, or there is a demand that the present life look like the past. All of these postures represent judgments and controls on the integration process and rejection of the present-time life experience as the container for past knowledge. The past is what must change and fit the present. Only the present-time life experience has sufficient energy to integrate the knowledge and experience from before.

Being in present time is necessary because **formlessness is only a present-time experience**—it cannot be felt or worked with if the individual slips back into past time and acts from old fixed structures. I can avoid the experience (and the anxiety) of formlessness if I am back in my old reactions, but in doing so I stop the changes that might occur and block the process of movement into new organizations. It is only in the present that I can be in the question and ask for answers about what I am feeling, what I need, or what I might do. Reorganization requires embracing what is happening right now.

Choices about creating are made in the present. To allow blending to occur requires the ability to handle formlessness because change is happening out of one's control.

Multidimensionality is another important feature of healthy structures that makes healing possible. Being in present time means that the individual's maximum level of consciousness is available to work with his or her wounded places. One can bring all of who one is to the process—physical aliveness, emotional strengths, spiritual knowledge, and relational connections to alter the state of one's bodymind. The individual can feel many emotional states and not just a single one. Adaptive thinking can be used to see solutions and reframe experience. Health includes the ability to do many things at once and blend them together. Both health and unhealth can be consciously experienced. Both physical and spiritual energies can be brought to the healing process. One is able to bring all that one knows and who one is to touch the past and forward the healing. Multidimensionality also means that the different aspects of the individual are aware of each other (co-consciousness) and all are considered in the process. The present-time moment is the integration and connection of all the levels of the bodymind, and healing can begin in as many of those levels as are able to be touched. The experience of trauma either reduces the number of states and dimensions in which an individual operates or it shifts those states away from bodily experience and the emotions. Health is about restoring multidimensionality to self experience and deepening the capacity for contact.

The creation of health is something that has to be perpetually chosen, especially during the healing process itself. **Moments of healing occur when connection is allowed between the wound structures that have been living in the past and the healthy structures of thought, feeling, and action that live in the present.** Large shifts in belief systems, physiological functioning and relationality occur when both the painful past and the alive energy of the present can coexist in the healing moment. The imagery and feelings of the trauma are now viewed from the perspective of the mature, healthy adult. Blending can occur when these two perspectives meet and the healthy side is sufficient to contain the movements of the past-time, uncontained traumatic experiences.

Many individuals have only limited abilities to retain states of present-time consciousness. Emotional trauma and the defenses they create leave bodies more solid, and subtract from the physical vitality necessary to stay vibrant. **The creation and support of present-time states of being is essential for an individual to be able to work with his or her unhealthy states.** An anchoring in these healthy states is the only way an individual can come back from despair, hopelessness, fear, or shame. Present-time healthy states are those that allow the emotions to be contained and not run wild. Present-time states of being are able to receive support, connect to sources of nurturance, choose what to do, and be creative and caring. To live in present time means being able to be interconnected—to use the strength and energy of the WE instead of just oneself alone. **The cohesive forces that allow the healthy sides of the self to develop are choice and interdependence. Choice is an act of consciousness, and interdependence means that blending has been learned.** Healing, then, can occur over time as vitality increases and more of the unhealthy structures can be faced.

Sustaining periods of healthy functioning also requires extending connections to the entire physical world. The vitality of the physical body cannot be maintained or increased without connection to the life that surrounds it in nature, and without that vitality, it is difficult to maintain those states of consciousness that heal deep patterns in the body or connect to larger spiritual realities.

Different levels of health are required for the different stages of psychospiritual growth. Figure 4 showed the kinds of healthy structures that, if developed, greatly facilitated the healing process. These are examples of some "core skills" needed to participate in the healing of emotional wounds. Still different structures of energy movement are required for sustained connection to spiritual reality, including the movement of Kundalini and more extensive grounding in the body[1].

Unlike many defensive and isolating structures, what is healthy in us always changes because it contains the possibilities of formlessness. Healthy connections to the many levels of the physical and etheric worlds require shifts and changes. These connections are far more formless than those of control or possession. They involve reevaluating and participating in keeping them alive and include the ability to move with knowledge—to act on what we know and note the impact of our actions.

Bringing Up the Dark Side

A question was asked in an earlier chapter—"Why do I have to feel all the negative stuff in order to change? Why can't I just move forward and do the new behaviors?" Making clear choices requires consciousness. Consciousness is the beginning of allowing the old self structures to have less force and control. Isolating and destructive behaviors structures change when touched by consciousness of a certain kind (especially that of acceptance), and each time this happens more health can be created. Then, more of the fixed and stagnant patterns in the psyche can be brought up for examination. **Structures must be made conscious before they can be released. In the healing process, release, emotional and**

bodily awareness, being in present time, receiving new answers, and choosing new options are all part of the same conscious movement. This movement entails the coming forward of healthier/more multidimensional parts of the self to touch the fixed forms that prevent full contact and expression. The process of bringing up the dark sides of the self into consciousness opens the door for reorganization to occur. Creating new forms for connection keeps the door open.

In Chapter 4, distinctions were made between the different structures that make up our experience of the dark side. Some were experiences and networks of memories that were unconscious and in shadow; others were defensive structures, fantasy structures, or possession levels. Healing requires increasing consciousness of all of these experiences, since all must be brought into the field of consciousness and choice. One of the painful parts of bringing the darker structures into awareness is that they often do not have choice as part of their structure. They are the parts within the self structure that have been separated from the whole and sometimes represent the consolidation of very destructive wishes. Most often they are reactions based on pain in which we become absorbed with little consciousness. For example, withdrawal, isolation, rage, revenge, taking, and controlling, are all very similar in their emergence. There is no awareness of their impact; strong denial about their presence; and pain associated with their expression. Just feeling and knowing that one is in these states requires considerable work in mindfulness. This awareness is a good beginning; it is necessary before one can change the dark-side structures or work very successfully with their outcome. There is often so much guilt and shame about our darker parts that even a little awareness of how they are being acted out will create a rush to suppression and a not wanting to know.

Another important reason for bringing the dark

sides of the self into conscius awareness is that there is always a "negative blending" of thoughts, feelings, and movements that must be separated before healing can occur. Shame is often woven together with anger, despair with reaching out for connection. Strong and healthy parts of the self have sometimes been hidden, judged, or linked with hopelessness. Developing the healthy parts of the self needed for healing means that they must be first separated from the judgments and controls established in the past.

The process of blending requires that the parts being blended all have movement and life, and seek connection. This is, of course, not true of all the dark-side structures that have been described. Structures of feeling and behavior that seek isolation and destruction (the defenses) rarely have life. Their function is to dampen and control connection and avoid the bursts of life energy that accompany change. Structures that support "staying the same" or controlling others rarely support life. As I described earlier, the energies, emotions, and beliefs of the wounds that lie under the defenses or lie hidden from consciousness have the most life, even though they are living in past time. They are relatively more formless (spontaneous) in their expression even though they consist of the irrational beliefs and the strong emotions of the past. They support connection, even if that connection is immature and reactive. **Thus, the core of the blending process as it occurs in healing brings the movements and belief structures of the wound together with the healthy side of the individual in the present time moment.** The defensive patterns, the fantasies, and the possessions have to be choicefully surrendered in order for this to occur. This direct access to the most painful parts of the dark side takes a great deal of courage for anyone to attempt. The healing is best done under conditions in which support is available and strengths can be accessed.

Interweaving

I have been describing a picture of the blending process as it happens in many forms of emotional healing. In this process, **healthy structures of the person—those patterns of thinking, moving, and relating that embody acceptance, responsibility, and choice—are used to touch the structures of the dark side and then the emotional wounding experience. This process creates releases that enable old patterns to complete themselves or dissolve, and allow the new answers and the energies of formlessness to emerge. Questions can be asked and solutions can be formed.** This healing process is seen again and again in emotional therapeutic work[2]. The actual techniques of blending can include listening with compassion and acceptance in someone's moment of need; telling healing stories using metaphors or images that resonate with the individual's needs; utilizing formal "rescripting" processes (such as those used in hypnosis, EMDR, or EEG Neurofeedback[2]); using imagery to connect someone to his or her personal sources of health; questioning dysfunctional beliefs to facilitate other ways of thinking about a problem; or helping produce more vital energetic processes in the body to replace the reactions of fear and contraction. The interweaving of healthier and more connected ways of being into the traumatized and wounded spaces is the essence of the healing experience. It occurs when the old structures can shift and new adaptive ways of thinking emerge; more expressive body movements take the place of freezing reactions and collapse; and when the touch of another can break through the isolation and aloneness of the wounded child.

It is important that some part of the structures to be blended be consciously present in the moments of healing. If the wounds or dark-side structures are not "lit up" or present, the healthier modes cannot penetrate the shell of isolation and blend as effectively. No choice is possible when these self structures are hidden from consciousness. Many individuals possess a large repertoire of healthy knowledge or movement abilities that result from extensive therapeutic experience, but do not feel that they were changed very much by these experiences. Often this is because the dark-side structures were never named, the wounds never exposed, and the healthy knowledge was never utilized to blend with those structures. Affirmations and other statements used to support health often cannot move into the dark-side structures unless the defenses are named, felt, and released, and the wounding is allowed to be consciously present. In the terminology of bodymind states, **blending requires that the original state in which the trauma or wound was created must be accessed in order for the new information to be linked and blended**. Healing childhood trauma requires access to childhood bodymind states. To change deep psychospiritual beliefs, access to earlier and even deeper patterns of life choices is necessary. When this accessing occurs, and when new solutions emerge that are related to the earlier patterns, blending is maximized.

The requirement that these healing moments occur in present time means that the therapist or healer must be able to bring present time to those parts of the wounded self that the client cannot. Our wounded places live in the past, and often we cannot bring present-time knowledge and healing into those spaces ourselves. To **hold present time** in the field of healing when strong emotional or destructive movements are occurring is a skill that experienced therapists have and continue to develop. It is the most essential of all the blending processes. Often the client can summon his or her own acceptance when the therapist cannot, and can also allow release to occur, but being in the wound and being in present time simultaneously is difficult if not impossible

Many systems of healing that incorporate blending

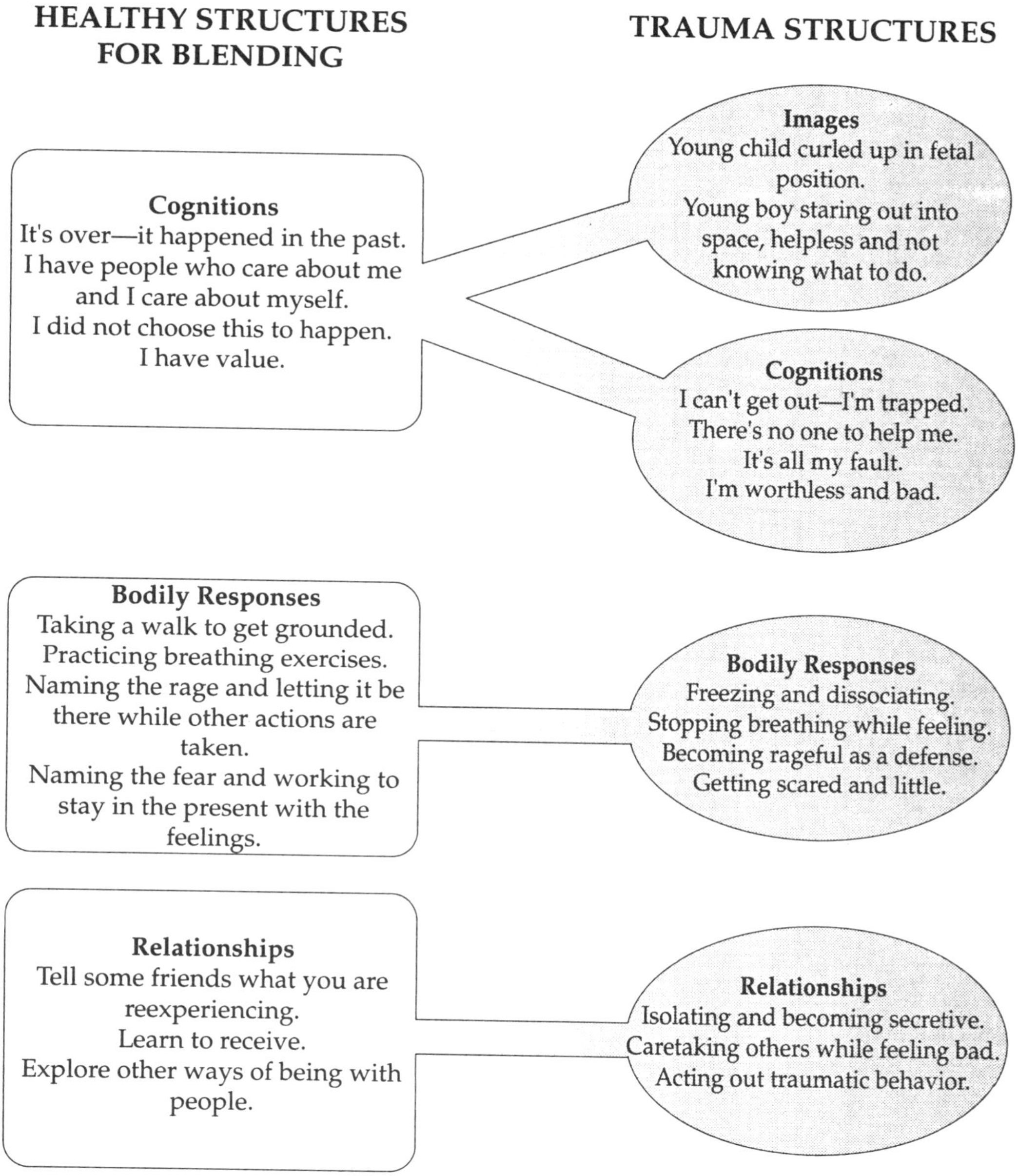

HEALTHY STRUCTURES FOR BLENDING

TRAUMA STRUCTURES

Images
Young child curled up in fetal position.
Young boy staring out into space, helpless and not knowing what to do.

Cognitions
It's over—it happened in the past.
I have people who care about me and I care about myself.
I did not choose this to happen.
I have value.

Cognitions
I can't get out—I'm trapped.
There's no one to help me.
It's all my fault.
I'm worthless and bad.

Bodily Responses
Taking a walk to get grounded.
Practicing breathing exercises.
Naming the rage and letting it be there while other actions are taken.
Naming the fear and working to stay in the present with the feelings.

Bodily Responses
Freezing and dissociating.
Stopping breathing while feeling.
Becoming rageful as a defense.
Getting scared and little.

Relationships
Tell some friends what you are reexperiencing.
Learn to receive.
Explore other ways of being with people.

Relationships
Isolating and becoming secretive.
Caretaking others while feeling bad.
Acting out traumatic behavior.

Figure 5. Some "Wounded Child" Structures and the Blends that were used in Healing

The Wound and Defenses   Healthy-Side Structures

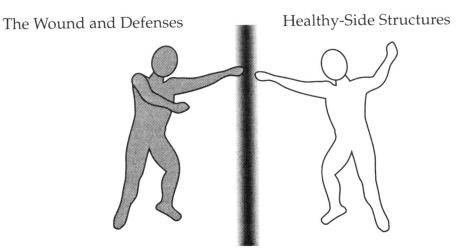

6a: Healthy knowledge that cannot touch the wound
because of the defenses. The wound remains
isolated and becomes darker over time.

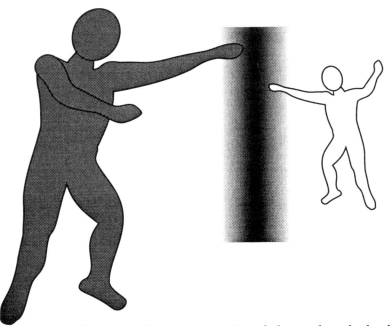

6b: The wound has more emotional charge than the healthy side
and would overwhelm the individual if allowed expression.
Health has to be built before blending can occur.

Figure 6. Unsuccessful Scenarios for Blending

require that the client use quite precise wording or specific movements for working with the shift from an unhealthy belief system into a healthier way of being. Larger descriptions of mental or physical dysfunction do not provide enough information on which to base a healing. For example, "depression" is not specific enough for the blending process—one does not blend with one's depression. The specific belief systems, memories, and somatic patterns that created and maintain the depression must come to consciousness to create the conditions for healing. Blending is essentially a mathematical process and the equations of health must be close to those that maintained non-health.

Figures 5 and 6 illustrate some of the principles of blending and an example of the healing process for trauma. Figure 5 is a representation of a trauma structure, and shows the different components of a "wounded child" self structure formed from a traumatic childhood experience. It shows the cognitive, imaginal, bodily, and relational components that emerged during therapy. Figure 5 also shows some of the sentences used and the movements done that were helpful in working with each component of the trauma structures and blending these structures into the healthy side. The blending process involves bringing more and more material to consciousness; it allows a reframing of the traumatic events by disorganizing the defensive patterns; allows feelings to be named, accepted, and choicefully expressed or contained; allows the emergence of new solutions; and allows impact by others for support and caring. In this process neither health nor unhealth is destroyed, but both are changed. Some of these interweaves immediately change the experience of the trauma structure, while others can take some time to alter response patterns. Continuing to reinforce the healthy bodymind structures while the dark side is being experienced serves to strengthen health, integrate it with the wound, and further disorganize the fixed nature of both the defensive and wound structures.

Figure 6 illustrates what happens when blending cannot occur. In 6a the healthy and unhealthy sides are kept separate through resistance or insufficient therapeutic help. In an earlier chapter, I mentioned situations in which dark-side and isolative parts of the self seem to take on a life of their own and not be accessible to choiceful processes. It is not uncommon for the dark sides of the inner child to appear to refuse blending—to want to stay hurt or angry or spoiled or passive. It is only after these positions have been under the scrutiny of consciousness for some time and the limiting nature of their attitudes experienced that they can yield some and begin blending.

Figure 6b illustrates a situation that occurs if there is not sufficient health to do the blending process. In this case, the charge and/or directions of the dark side are much too great for the current healthy skills of the person to handle, and he or she is at risk of being overwhelmed with depression, rage, fear, or self-destruction. There must be much more mobilization of health along the lines of support, information, or body experience for blending to happen.

It is important in blending (healing) work that the individual stay close to his or her sources of strength during the process. Maintaining connection to support systems, continually reinforcing one's strengths, and building health in the body are necessary for the process to have a good outcome. The ability to hold visions of health, sustain a new worldview, and keep the connection to sources of energy is necessary to continue the blending over time. This is the process of building attractor structures for nourishing the healthy energies that support change. Once the dark side has been brought up, the individual enters a space where choice has not been established, perhaps ever, and the possibility of freezing and isolating or avoiding and denying is very present. Blending is done consciously—riding the edge of those wounded places—and all the available tools of awareness and choice are applied. Strong emotions live in those spaces and exhaustion is not very far away.

It is important that solutions remain formless and available for change. Often the individual does not know how to behave differently or what thinking patterns will be effective on a given day. New ways of being are constantly created and there is never one thing that works for every situation. Be in the question, ask people for help, try different ways of moving, seek new knowledge. Answers that emerge are worth trying and some will form the basis for later, more enduring healthy patterns. It is better to act and choose and move than to wait for the perfect solution. Both bodies and minds are strengthened by doing.

In Chapter 3, a model for the change process was discussed—the **Formula for Change**. The steps in this model also describe the basic blendings that occur as part of healing:

Acceptance: Naming emerging energies and behaviors as they come into consciousness; regarding what emerges with acceptance and working with the judgments that come up; developing the **witness function** (the ability to be an observer to all aspects of thought, emotional response, and action as a first step in bringing choice into self-movements); touching those dark structures with both heart and mind and without judgment.

Responsibility: Taking responsibility for what you are doing and what you would like to change; separating from your issues and answers to see what can be changed; discerning what is yours and what is not.

Release: Allowing feelings to flow and change to occur; allowing and fostering the emergence of new answers and new self-organizations.

Change: Consciously choosing other ways to be; acting on the answers being received and fostering new connections to the external world; shaping new responses to old triggers and developing new patterns of behavior and new skills; speaking your truth and showing yourself in the world.

These steps are the working processes for healing old wounds and changing. The process is always limited by what the individual is able to move toward and accept, and how much he or she is able to work with. Step by step the structures emerge and are blended and integrated into the healthy side. In this way the past is slowly brought into the present. Trauma then exists as a memory but not as an energized structure operating in the present. That energy has been captured by the present-time healthy structures and bound with choice.

Figure 7 shows in pictorial form the stages of the Formula for Change and the different blends that the change process comprises.

Figure 8 is still another way to view the Formula for Change. It describes how the model can be linked to the organic process of pulsation, and blends the stages of Acceptance and Responsibility with the processes of metabolism, and the stages of Release and Change with those of organizing form and connecting to the world.

There are, of course, many levels at which healings (as blendings) can occur, both in therapeutic work and in psychospiritual growth. New information can come from within the self as well as from many sources external to the individual. Following are some common examples:

Blendings within the Self: This group includes many of the examples I have already mentioned and includes all healing processes in which healthy parts of the self are mobilized to challenge defenses and enter past-time wound structures. Examples include chang-

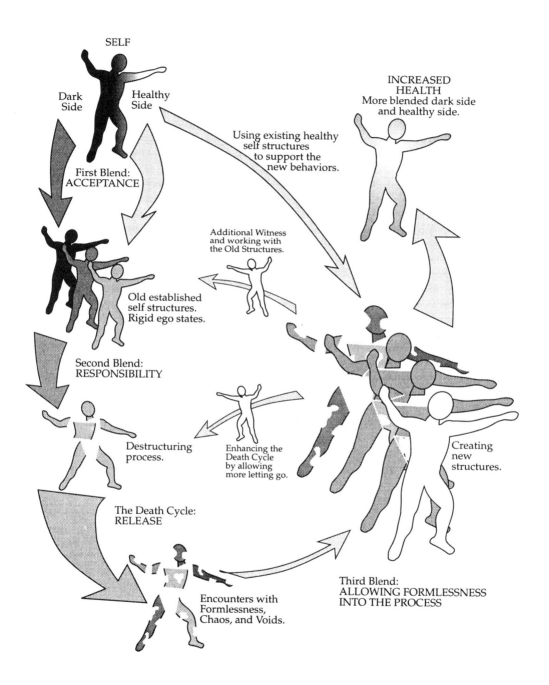

Figure 7. Living in the Question

The Formula for Change is a model of the change process that parallels observations of pulsatory movement in living systems. These models describe creative processes, transformational change, and reorganization as having two basic phases—an **instroke** (an inhalation) in which there is movement from periphery to core, and an **outstroke** (an exhalation) of movement from core to periphery (see Muller-Schwefe, 1994). In the instroke, we take the world into our core, and to do that we need the abilities described in the phases of Acceptance and Responsibility—to allow contact with acceptance, see and know without judgment, name energies to make them more conscious, and participate with responsibility. In these phases, energetic charge develops and our participation in the process of receiving allows the energy of contact to be converted to something that is "ours" and can be gathered into our core. Since we cannot always control what impacts us, acceptance is a necessary attitude to be able to organize a healthy response to whatever is touched. Learning to receive what we cannot control, allowing touch by a greater range of energies, and learning to separate out toxic from nurturant experiences are necessary so we can take in the energy and information to create a new response. In the outstroke, energy moves outward, emotions are released, and organization for contact takes place. In the Formula, the phases of Release and Change describe the abilities formed in outstroke processes. These phases describe the movement from self to world—letting our insides touch the outside, in discharging emotions, forming new behaviors for connection, and expressing our truth and purpose. These connections, in turn, form the basis for the new inputs. The many experiences of formlessness (e.g., chaos, voids, space, or the challenge of living in the present) can occur in any phase of this process— for example, anywhere a function is missing due to lack of development; at the "turning points" where instroke becomes outstroke (and vice versa) and new answers might emerge; where the discharge cannot be contained; if reorganization is not complete; or when we are touched by something new or something very formless. The Formula for Change also describes how blending must occur in all phases of the cycle for healing to be complete, and not just in the instroke or the outstroke cycles. The cycle of transformation is circular, with all phases touching all the others in the moment of reorganization.

Figure 8. The Formula for Change, the Breath of Life, and the Inside and Outside of the Self

ing one's thought patterns from judgment to acceptance (learning to explore one's behavior and feelings without judgment); moving and breathing differently in stressful situations (learning to utilize bodymind skills to walk through difficult emotional experiences with more choice); and taking the needs of the wounded child within that were fixed by deprivation or neglect and expressing them in an adult mode (moving with your consciousness into the "trance states" of the wounded child to modify their expression). These blendings also include many forms of spiritual exercises in which diverse parts of the self are brought together—for example, blending the heart and feelings with thinking, blending mind (consciousness) and body, blending soul and body, blending one's past with one's present, and so forth.

Blendings with Outside Sources of Connection: This group includes allowing connection with external sources of energy, support, healing, or consciousness to allow another way of being to emerge or become organized. Examples include accepting support, either through touch or emotional caring, in order to walk through (learn a new response to) a crisis or an emotional event; participating in energy work that will allow your own body to alter its characteristic way of being and move to a new plateau; using biofeedback or entrainment devices to alter your state; or deepening your connection to the world of nature or spirit (learning to connect and blend with other life forms or energetic patterns). For true blending to occur, the individual must be able to fully participate in the process. Otherwise, possession is a risk. In these examples, the energies with which you blend are either eventually removed (as in accepting a healing by another person—the healer impacts you, removes their presence, and leaves you in a different state), or, you become a part of some larger energetic system and have to make new choices about what to do with the new connection. Working with the Kundalini energy of the planet and developing mediumship are psychospiritual examples of the latter type of blending. Significant shifts occur in the individual's energy system as a result of blending with these types of energetic systems and one is permanently altered by the process.

In the above examples there are differences in the size of the structural shifts and in the energies of the healthy side needed to do the tasks. Some shifts occur in only one phase of the Formula for Change, while others involve taking the process through the entire range of movement. More energy is mobilized in larger shifts and larger shifts take more aliveness to maintain. Certain kinds of psychospiritual work (such as the altered states in which connections to other realities are cultivated) take high levels of energy and preparation. Psychic readings, energy healing, and deep states of meditation seem to be best done and maintained if the body is healthy and can run its energy well.

These shifts in structure can take lots of time or can happen very quickly. Many wonderful surprises occur in this work and it is hard to predict what will emerge once the process begins. Some individuals get new solutions quickly, but have difficulty maintaining the health and energy necessary to sustain the new behaviors. Others are slow to form new structures, but keep them very alive. Some healers try to provide answers to help structures form; others make more space and are willing to wait for the new answers to emerge. Some individuals can work with those formless places in which there are no apparent answers yet; some people try to get organized as quickly as possible. Each of us heals and transforms in our own way.

Enhancing Experiences

The blending process is also seen in many bodymind

exercises in which sources of positive, vital energy are "sourced" to enhance performance or strengthen the spiritual health of the individual. Specific disciplines can be practiced in which compassion, courage, relaxation, humor, determination, acceptance, hope, will, wisdom, power, enthusiasm, optimism, mindfulness, unity, nonviolence, and so forth, are brought into the body and blended with the bodymind of the individual. If these forms and energies do not exist in strength within the person, they must be first accessed through outside sources. The blending process here involves making these experiences more conscious (more accessible by choice), and learning how to cultivate them as sources of strength and knowledge. These energies are also used to enhance the execution of future tasks, such as specific performances, the healing of illnesses, or making one's way through difficult life passages.

In the range of experiences called spiritual emergencies, an individual might have an unexpected infusion of energies that are initially very disruptive to current levels of understanding, emotional balance, or physical health. Having a Kundalini opening, a near-death experience, the realization of clairvoyance or mediumship, or a spiritual experience like touching the Christ-Force or some other essence can be a challenge to what one is able to blend with and integrate into one's current self experience. Sometimes these energies create massive changes in thought systems, in emotional functioning, or in the state of the body, and maintaining what has been shifted is also a blending process. It is necessary to move toward such shifts and participate in the new states. Such potential transformations of self experience can be aborted if there is unprocessed dark-side material that comes up and is then suppressed; if the person cannot complete the releases that occur with the touch of the new energies; if there are no new behaviors (new ways to act) created to contain the new energies; or if there is no support for the new learnings. The lack of movement in any stage of the Formula for Change can stop the transformation process.

Many levels of blending occur as healing progresses and psychospiritual development proceeds. **The blending process is the basic way in which the bodymind is transformed and the spiritual life can be embraced.** Increasing the vitality of the body and changing the self experience involves blending the different aspects of the self with one another as well as with the energies and essences that live around each of us. The science of blending is the modern equivalent of alchemy and represents one foundation of the transformation process.

Polarities

Psychospiritual work differs from healing in that the work requires an increasing focus on subtle movements within the bodymind, and the ability to work more and more abstractly. Both of these types of movements represent more formless ways of interacting with the world—one by working with *energetic flows* felt deeply in the body and the other by working with *abstract concepts* of a spiritual nature. Spiritual experience must include both, since both the structures of the body and mind underlie the self experience. Spiritual knowledge assists in the shifting of belief systems about the world, and in opening to the search for experiences that would not ordinarily be sought after. Working with the body opens the perceptual abilities so the connection can happen.

In the following section, I will try to describe an application of the blending process to spiritual work. It reflects what I have learned from the process so far, but surely does not exhaust its possibilities. It is difficult to write about—initially, the energetic movements are subtle and the outcomes so formless that there is often a fine line between imagining (visualizing) something happening and actually experiencing the structures that are forming. I hoped that by ending the material in this text with these exercises I might convey something of the broader application of the principles that I have been using in my healing work.

In the Teacher's classes, one part of the energy work rested on understanding and experiencing four different dualities or pulsatory movements:

Giving and Receiving
Life and Death
Inside and Outside
Positive and Negative

These polarities have very concrete aspects as well as larger metaphorical meanings. Like many spiritual concepts, they may be taken (and applied) literally, but on further investigation also seem to have many layers of meaning. Like self experience, each time it is contacted, something new and different arises—some new learning is possible. Like many other polarities that seem to carry spiritual meaning (for example, the yin-yang duality), these also may be understood in several ways:

•Each pole, in itself, represents a "way of being", an energy, or a process that can be seen and felt in the physical world. Since one of the goals of spiritual growth is to break down the articificial boundaries between the physical and subtle world—to bring form and formlessness together— each side of the duality also has a physical and subtle aspect. Working with dualities of any kind represents a process in which opposites are faced, positions are flipped, and the physical and energetic are seen as two sides of the same coin.

•Each pole taken by itself represents a split in our ability to function in the world—that is, if we only manifest one of the poles in our experience and behavior we are not complete, and the expressions become destructive rather than creative. The pulsatory movements of all living systems polarize when subject to sufficient stress. Instead of a fluid movement between two extremes, one side is fixated. Polarization prevents movements that might lead toward synthesis, integration, or the ability to reorganize at a different level and make more complex connections. Polarization means that systems of natural pulsation have been disturbed by trauma or neglect and the individual no longer can live in the full range of his or her possibilities.

•The two ends of the polarity represent a pulsation of energy flow and behavior that, if brought together, would bring completion to a creative process. The work involved in blending polarities is similar to the blending of darkside and healthy-side structures in healing. Both patterns are brought into consciousness and begin to shift as they touch each other. Opposites will never be the same; they will always have separate identities as experiences and processes in nature. The act of touching them together however, means that a pulsation can occur and energy can move. These movements represent the creative process in motion and bring life to the bodymind.

Giving and Receiving: Most trauma to the bodymind leaves the individual stuck in one or another of these poles. Usually, emotional wounds leave the individual with an energy system that is not well contained, and energy moves without choice out of the body and is lost. Sometimes the pattern of giving away energy gets covered up with a caretaker pattern, in which taking under the guise of giving becomes a way to restore the body. Addictions and stimulations become necessary and cycles of depletion alternate with stimulation or nurturance-seeking. Giving and receiving become separate forms of pursuit removed from conscious choice. The state of the body that underlies these patterns also remains unconscious. Opening these patterns to conscious examination is necessary for healing and for the building of aliveness to do spiritual work. Opening to receive must be part of healing—but one outcome of that experience may be to touch the losses of the past. In this case, receiving will be a struggle for a while, until those losses become processed and the body is able to open to outside touch. The maxim that "one cannot truly give except from fullness" is learned in this process as healthier states of bodymind awareness begin to govern both giving and receiving and replace previous beliefs about having to deserve gifts or being valued only for what one can give to others. Most wounded child ego states have strong judgments about what they deserve or what they must do to earn worth, and these beliefs strongly impact the health and vitality of the body by limiting both giving and receiving. If receiving can be felt as being touched by the world and giving as touching and expressing one's energy in the world, more balance can come into the energy equations of the body. Bringing these two polarities together means that a connection can be made with others in which all parties benefit from the exchange. Change is possible. Health builds as connections to the life around us builds, and both giving and receiving blend into more fluid patterns of connection.

Life and Death: There are many distortions that maintain this polarity, the most obvious of which are stances in which one is feared and the other treasured. Picturing death as the "grim reaper" and a negative outcome after a full life makes it difficult to bring the two together and see the two processes as equal partners in creation. In Western society, materiality is a dominant philosophical frame; it holds the position that life and self only exist in physical form. This makes physical death equal to loss of self and the enemy of life. Death becomes equated to the etheric world and is feared, while the only life processes that are valued are the ones we can see and feel.

Blending this polarity means that both life and death will be felt and seen as generative (both acting in the interest of creation), and that life in human form has both physical and etheric aspects. Touching the two as part of the life cycle keeps murder from occurring. It makes dying a process in which new life is created instead of destroyed. Putting something into the death cycle is a way of keeping it alive by restoring its etheric foundation—letting the physical aspects of the form change to reflect changes in the energetic patterns. Bringing something from death into life means bringing forth the energetic aspects into physical form. Back and forth, from form to energy and from energy to form.

The experience of physical dying is a part of every level of personal transformation—structures must change to encompass new energetic flows. At the most basic level, just letting go of old ways of being is a way of touching death—letting rigid and historical thought and action patterns die so a new form can make new connections to the world. This means surrendering identifications within the psyche and removing our basic attachment to beliefs, behavior patterns, emotions, and body as self. The new forms and answers that emerge come forth *because* death is present. In spiritual development, moving into more formless energetic experiences of life and self means touching death even more strongly and feeling its presence intermingled with the forces that create life. Death is not a stagnant energy. It shines, pulsates, moves, and creates life in whatever it touches. It is the separation of life and death that creates stagnation and rejects formlessness by rejecting the etheric world and the energetic source of our creativity. Touching life and death together means allowing the change cycle to complete itself. Dying and release can happen so new answers can emerge and behaviors form around them.

Inside and Outside: There are many ways in which this pulsation is reflected in healing and spiritual development. The infant's first self is the mother-child bond. We begin our life as a *We*, retreat (through trauma) to an *I*, and attempt to get back to a choiceful and conscious

We. In our experience, stillness and inner perception alternate with involvement and movement into the outer world. Inside and outside appear so different—one is to *be* and the other is to *do*. In our lives, periods of expansive creativity alternate with inner work. Inside and outside appear to be two separate domains separated by the skin and the boundary of an individual self.

But this polarity is another false dichotomy. The sense of a separate and isolated "me" or "I" is gradually replaced with a sense of self quite inseparable from surrounding life. Change becomes impossible without connection. The self does not form without contact. Healing cannot occur without an other. The structures that appeared to exist within are part of what they have connected to and been formed by. The deeper one goes into the psyche, the less personal the content becomes and the fewer boundaries are felt between self and universe. As we look more deeply within for self, we begin to experience a universe that is certainly not self, at least not the self we expected. The external world is also within. We are a clone of the planet and the heavens, inseparable from both. We make our own atmosphere, run the Kundalini, generate light, and share mindspace with all life everywhere. The only universe that exists for us is the one we bring forth through living with others. The only self that exists is the one we momentarily create by connection.

In personal growth work, all kinds of synchronicities begin to occur that also blur the distinction between inner and outer spaces. Students begin to see that their process is occurring all over the place, in all the people and processes to which they are connected. The more an individual allows the world to impact him or her, the more this occurs, until world and self begin to blend energetically. How much of this "unity consciousness" we can contact at any given moment depends on how much of that impact we can allow.

Bringing inner and outer together creates a movement in which our spiritual life gets lived in the world. We speak what we believe, we apply our principles to our lives, and we practice what we preach. Our external movements follow from our internal ones, and we begin to allow ourselves to be touched in ways that go into our core.

Negative and Positive: The duality "negative and positive" refers to actual electrical activity in the bodymind as well as the more general problem of how physical and energetic connections are made and maintained. The bodymind's ability to grow, expand, differentiate, and create new avenues for connection to the world is reflected in the movement of electrical activity in the brain and body systems and in the atomic structure of each cell. Negative and positive ions and electrons must continue to connect and disconnect for movement to occur. In the larger sense, these physcial systems reflect the constant need for energy and direction to meet and maintain their connection. They are not always together. We can have lots of energy, but no direction. We can desire connection, but have no energy. Our knowledge, purpose, and inner wisdom can lie fallow without the passion and energy to move. We can use our energy to follow other's directives and never choose to find our own path.

Having spiritual direction means connecting to our inner wisdom—our potential—giving it time to flower and mature, and finding places where it can be expressed. That is the positive pole. The negative pole is the energetic aspect of this process—claiming the passion and caring, and working with the resistance and fear that comes with allowing the innermost parts of the self to touch the external world. Blending positive and negative means connecting our feelings to our purpose, harnessing the energies of the emotions and the body to the healthiest parts of the self experience.

The first goal of the blending process with these dualities is to touch, feel, and accept both polarities. This means touching one's weaknesses and voids, places where there is no development of one side or the other. Each side becomes known and felt as a separate experience. Becoming aware of difficulties in Receiving, releasing the fears and blocks to the experience of Death, working/expressing in the Outside World, or bringing the emotions into present time, might be the goals of such work for some people. The Formula for Change describes the stages through which these efforts pass. Like healing work, in which the dark side, the wound, and the healthy functions must be present in consciousness, both poles of each duality must be known and embraced. Many schools of personal development teach these principles, and there are many ways to learn the behaviors necessary to develop these movements.

Blending them together means being able to move back and forth within each duality and experience both poles in a pulsatory movement. Sometimes they are felt together, as if they are the same process. Mostly they alternate, each having its own feeling and expression. When they are blending and feel like part of the same movement, there is a creative vitality in the experience— a feeling of flow and completeness, and a certain sense of potential and possibility. Moving fluidly between the poles of any of these dualities—Giving and Receiving, Life and Death, Inside and Outside, or Positive and Negative—enhances the connection with others, with one's own body, and within one's own body. Each of these cycles has a certain feeling that occurs when the movements are fluid. Like the new solutions that emerge in healing moments, these processes release energy, create a sense of vitality in the body, and open visions for other ways to be that did not exist before.

The final step in the process is to do something with the answers that emerge. The stage of *Change* in the Formula for Change reflects the need to complete the cycle of creation by moving toward connection and interaction with the world. What should I do with this vitality? Which paths should I pursue? Growth is completed through connection, and the impact of that connection in turn creates further questions.

The theme of this text has been that one of the most important goals of psychospiritual growth is to keep the change process moving by creating bodymind structures of thought, feeling, and action that can connect to the world and still hold formlessness as part of their structure. These attitudes and behaviors allow approaches to life problems that can hold acceptance, move with responsibility, allow release, and create forms that can hold change as a permanent possibility. This means that the forms (the behaviors themselves) are not important in themselves but exist only as temporary carriers of purpose and identity. As new information and consciousness emerge, the old answers become a base for the next question. This is how systems, like an alive self, stay aligned with all Life and continue to evolve.

Chapter 9

Living in the Question

*Living in the Question is a way of talking about the
end product of a series of personal transformations
in which formlessness has been experienced
and integrated into the psyche.*

A s I have proposed several times in this essay,
one of the fundamental skills that needs to
be learned in psychospiritual work is the ability
to change—to allow oneself to be impacted by the world
and to participate in the experience choicefully. This
means that formlessness in all of its different aspects is
touched, and the movements between questions and
answers, knowing and uncertainty, direction and chaos,
become less frightening and can be more fully embraced.
Although schools of spiritual development differ widely
in their content and their purposes, all seem to share the
movement toward allowing more formlessness into the
lives of their students.

The effort required to allow formlessness into one's
habits of thinking and behavior could certainly be called
a struggle. Most situations in which there are problems
require answers—becoming organized, being certain. We
are caught and challenged by forms everywhere. Habits and routine behaviors are more efficient, easier to do,
and form the basis for competence. Knowing has a higher

value in our culture than experiencing, and sitting with a question over time is something that is rarely taught. Uncertainty creates an uneasiness, a press to come up with something and not sit there in the void for too long. Do something! Adding to the difficulty for some is a history of trauma associated with feeling helpless and not having a way to act. This makes it harder to touch formlessness and explore its many faces.

Living in the Question allows the faces of formlessness to be a conscious part of the spiritual growth process. Psychospiritual development fosters completeness; the struggle is to touch the structures of the self within and extend outward to the world. When this is done, we become complete. Energy moves in the creative cycle and structures are formed that enhance the self. Living in the Question does not mean that answers are not valued or energy does not need to be organized into action. The opposite is true. Answers and action form the basis for further movement and further questions. Living in the Question does mean that those answers never get written in stone—that the process of creating the answer moves with what is occurring, and as it proceeds it shapes itself around the situation. Bringing formlessness, space, and openness into one's personal life brings more breadth and depth to one's responses. Being defensive, isolated, judgmental, ritualistic, and unconscious is acting rigidly and in fixed forms. When one is Living in the Question, one can respond to a larger order, include more connections, and embrace more energy and life. Cooperation and harmony are more formless than control and possession. Considering self and others together is more formless than either one alone. Bringing self to touch nature and spiritual reality requires more formlessness than living in isolation.

Learning to Question

Asking questions is an art with a science backround. Asking a question is a way of negotiating new experiences and a method of looking for a way to respond and connect more deeply. The goal of a question is to create a form, and the quality, intent, and form of the question goes a long way toward determining what kind of form is created. Answers can be demanded, requested, pleaded for, avoided, or severely limited by the nature of the question. I can ask for answers from a victim place, from a neutral place, from a hostile place, or from a state of acceptance and compassion. The energy in and around a question is a part of the question. Questions can challenge forms, disorganize people, open up issues for a new perception, or imply other dimensions of experience waiting to be acknowledged. To see a question work is to see the energy of formlessness touch structure, and to see possibility touch existing reality. Bringing a question to a problem provides the opportunity to begin the process of change—to stimulate the witness, to take responsibility, to let go of old solutions, and to create new options. Questions work in each stage of the change process to help both receive the answers and form responses.

The experience of formlessness exists at all levels of the bodymind and as a part of many different phases of the change process. It can be a reaction to alterations in the structure of one's life; the goal is to accept the new loss of structure and begin again with questions. Formlessness can be a transitional stage of some length. Answers do not always leap forth when asked for and the creation of some self structures can take years. Yielding up the beliefs of one's childhood or the karmic patterns of one's history can take many years of conscious work. Formlessness can also be a tool. It can be used to cultivate behaviors that challenge rituals and fixed ways of

being, and help one to become more and more practiced
in moving through cycles of change. Formlessness is the
partner of change, and the more one allows change, the
more formlessness will appear in the corners of one's experience.

Uncertainty

There is something intrinsically unreasonable about
the cultivation of formlessness, since one of its consequences is an increase in uncertainty—putting less em-
phasis on the answer, and spending more time and energy with the question. Uncertainty is usually a stres-
sor and almost always results in attempts to increase control and predictability, and in a greater need for feed-
back. The cultivation of formlessness, therefore, has to
overcome a very basic need of the individual to gain back
certainty about life and direction. This need greatly increases people's reliance on any social or psychological
systems that can provide answers. Psychics, religious
groups, therapists, and so forth are consulted heavily in
times of personal or social stress when uncertainty is
high, since answers help—even if they are not always
understood or fully examined. The human need to make
meaning out of life means that answers will be sought
and created whenever voids are experienced.

The experience of Living in the Question is brought
gradually into one's life. Formlessness can be embraced
as health and connectivity build. For most individuals,
already-established answers and solutions are brought
to their life problems, and they are willing to tolerate
some uncertainty while events unfold. If one has a basi-
cally stable and cohesive self experience, it is easier to
question other aspects of one's beliefs and actions. Formlessness "chips away" at our solid forms and begins to
shift the center of our beingness from external roles and

fixed patterns to internal states and more fluid ways of responding to the world. There are pulsations, back and forth from question to answer, from letting go of answers to creating new behaviors, from knowing to uncertainty. Increasing one's movement along those dimensions is how formlessness can be cultivated. Learning to accept the lack of control we have over many aspects of our lives, learning to respond to new events in a healthier way, reaching out for more connections to others, and learning to let go more gracefully, are all ways to cultivate the presence of questions. Formlessness can best be explored from positions of safety and from states of cohesiveness. The better our connections to the world, the more risk we can take in letting them go and exploring how they might become even better.

Healing

Allowing formlessness into the self experience means that states of chaos and personal voids can be touched consciously, named and altered, if desired, with choice. It means that connections can begin to be made where none existed before. It means that the fear of chaos and those isolated empty spaces within the self can be walked through with compassion and caring, and questions can be asked where no structure of any kind existed before. It means that those periods of uncertainty and unknowing can be walked through with more gentleness, with a sense of what kind of support is needed, and with the ability to use the stable and healthy parts of the self or connections to others to provide strength for the journey.

Healing is a series of acts in which healthy parts of the self are brought together with structures that have remained untouched—those unblended places within the self whose forms have held pain, loss, helplessness and isolation. The emotions associated with those structures run wild, and are not connected to purposes that promote life. When first contacted and brought to consciousness, these are extreme states. Formlessness is present in states of chaos and voids, and form is present in defenses and in connections that are rigid, ritualistic, mechanical, and limited. Healing occurs in the creation of attitudes and connections to others that bring in energy and life and allow more generous and graceful exchanges with the world. Order is brought to chaos as those connections are formed.

Bringing questions to the process of healing means challenging old and seemingly fixed negative beliefs about the self and world. Can I change? Do I deserve to be cared about? Will you help me? Is it safe to express myself in the world? Can I have what I want? These are the questions of the wounded child. Challenging these beliefs and behaviors with possibilities of other ways of being represents the healing process.

For the healer, bringing formlessness into the healing process means participating in the flow of the client's energy. It means not having the answer for the client, but helping each person find his or her own answer by supporting him or her in the process of change. Introducing formlessness means teaching acceptance, encouraging responsibility, providing support in periods of release, and celebrating the emergence of new answers and self structures that can connect in a healthier way to the world.

Connecting to the World

Allowing formlessness into the self experience means that the behaviors we do create for connecting to the world have more fluidity—that they are able to maintain connections with others that allow others to change as well. It means that we allow ourselves to be impacted and perhaps changed by what we connect to, that our connections to others are less controlling and more allowing of their reality. Uniqueness and individuality are appreciated, since forms are less important than the substances they hold. It means we can coexist with others, celebrate their lives, and give to ourselves through those connections.

Allowing formlessness into relationships is the practice of blending. Blending entails making connections while being open to the possibility of change. It means being able to stay connected to energies and attitudes in others that previously might have elicited judgment or avoidance. Blending means being able to be with others in their moments of chaos, fear, anger, hatred, or pain, and bring other attitudes and energies into the field— not necessarily to agree, but to make contact and have a response. Questions about blending involve asking, "How can I move better with this situation? How can I stay connected and still have my own feelings and movements? How can I participate here and bring my energy into the process?"

Selfhood

Allowing formlessness into the self experience means that one's own personal self experience can contain emptiness as well as content—that the vast field of mind can be experienced as well as the thoughts, feelings, sensations, and specific realities that move across its surface. It means that the self experience reflects more of life and creation, and is constantly shifting and moving. Multiple self structures become opportunities for connection and blending. Instead of a commitment to reconstituting a familiar self experience at every turn, allowing formlessness into the self experience means that the process of change—the steps of the Formula for Change—becomes more embodied, less frightening. Acceptance, responsibility, release, and the creation of movement become more practiced and familiar. It means that we continue to live in present time—the most formless of states—instead of in the past or future.

Allowing formlessness also means that the self experience holds many more abstract and energetic aspects, moving the base of movement from the fixed ego structures that seem like machines into deeper, more fluid states and structures. Creativity can be a process that is blended with the self experience. New energies and forces can be allowed to be a part of what we think of as our self, and abundance can be embraced over safety. There is more awareness of the energy fields of the body, bodymind states such as value, courage, and compassion that provide the basis of new movements into the world, and soul experiences that bring the knowledge of one's individual purpose. We learn to act from different, deeper centers within the self. Allowing formlessness means that we begin responding more purposefully to energies within us—our needs, our talents, our dreams—and create the physical forms that hold those energetic connections sacred.

When one cultivates experiences of space and emptiness (such as those that form such an integral part of Buddhism and other spiritual traditions), one moves away from the experience of self as a set of fixed structures, identifications, and reaction patterns.[1] Cultivating the experience of space is a way of entering a field of experience without formed answers or conceptions of what will happen. It is like starting over each moment and witnessing the birth of new possibilities of being. These traditions put the self into the question and allow the individual to begin blending with the formless nature of spiritual reality.

Spirituality

Allowing formlessness into the self experience means that we are not so far from the mystery and sacredness of life. Forms are appreciated, but the energy behind, around, and through them are felt as well. Rituals, especially spiritual ones, are evaluated on the basis of what they create and what they help one achieve— what energies they contain as well as how they might look. Appreciating and cultivating formlessness means that we reach toward the etheric, intangible, imaginative, subtle, natural, and mysterious, and that we try to find ways to deepen and nourish our connections with those other, less solid worlds.

Allowing formlessness into one's spiritual life reflects a willingness to examine dogma wherever it occurs. It means making religion more spiritual. Like Abraham did, it means working with a more formless and abstract God—more difficult to make real, more difficult to touch and feel. It means that God is no longer a statue, no longer a specific form, but is behind and around a process of connection within the self and with the world. Allowing formlessness means taking old beliefs, historical truths, and firm principles, and putting them in the question. How do they work for me now? Are they inclusive or isolating? Do they support change in me? Are they life-affirming? Putting something in the question means looking at its symbolic and metaphorical aspects as well as its concrete existence. Allowing formlessness means reaching for higher levels of order and organization and seeking a connection to something more abstract, while not losing the connection to what is real and solid. It means blending the etheric with the physical and participating in the changes that result.

We seem to be in a period in our culture in which the forms around us are changing rapidly. Even something so stable as our grounding in the planet is shifting. The destruction of ecosystems, alterations in the atmosphere, shifting earth energies, and changes in cultural institutions bathe us in experiences of change without predictability. We are constantly impacted by such energetic changes and touched by the formlessness of the fields created by these shifts. We can respond by polarizing further or by embracing the attendant formlessness and learning how to question, accept others, and blend. The self grows by including the world in its structure and by Living in the Question about the outcome.

Glossary

There are several terms in this text associated with the process of psychospiritual development that may be unfamiliar to readers not involved in such pursuits. This glossary elaborates further on those concepts that are not covered in the text or the notes.

Clairvoyance - Clairvoyance is a psychic ability that allows perception of subtle (etheric) energy fields and the information that these fields contain. Clairvoyance (psychic seeing) is the most common psychic ability used in psychic readings and intuitive healing, although skilled individuals can also receive psychic information through clairaudience (psychic hearing) or clairsentience (psychic knowing/feeling). These abilities differ from mediumship in that they involve the *perception* of subtle energies, but not the channeling or movement of these energies *through* the bodymind. The range of possible psychic skills is great, and includes very primitive perceptions of emotional fields that are thought to be mediated by the autonomic nervous system as well as the highly developed extended sense perceptions of some individuals.

Energy - The term energy (as used in psychic and spiritual work) is utilized as a metaphor as well as a precise physical science term. The term is used to refer to a wide range of phenomena including psychophysiological changes in the body, the movement of the emotions, electromagnetic energies, the auric field around the body (a subtle energy), the atmospheres around living forms, the structure of non-physical reality, and the transmission of information between and within systems. Many of the referents for this term (e.g., etheric energy, chi energy, prana, or orgone energy) are not yet well substantiated by physics research, although they have been detected by human observers for centuries and are written about in many sacred traditions. In those instances in which it cannot be easily measured, the term *energy* may be used more as an explanatory concept awaiting future validation. The term energy can also be used to refer to the changing, fluid, formless aspects of a situation—the opposite of form or structure. In this text, I have used the word *energy* in several ways—as a term to describe what occurs when old structures of behavior are released and new internal movements in the body begin, as a way of describing the formless nature of spiritual reality, and as a tentative explanatory concept. I am aware that it may be confusing to use the same word to describe such different phenomena as "energy work" and "spiritual energy," but I have not found acceptable substitutes.

Energy work - There are many exercises that students of schools of spiritual development might use to further develop the capacities of the bodymind to perceive subtle internal movements and enter the world of spiritual experience. The Yogas of the East contain many of these, as do the Sufi traditions and the shamanic schools. Almost all these schools utilize visualization and breathing exercises as well as disciplines to open the senses, quiet the mind, open to outside sources of energy, and work in an altered state. The term *running energy* is also used to describe exercises that work with the body. The goal of these exercises is to help the body become *more physical* and *less solid (rigid)*, to bring consciousness and vitality to all aspects of bodily functioning. A related goal is to achieve a deeper blending of the physical body with etheric energy—toward developing the body as an organ of spiritual perception. Physical exercise is a part of these programs, as is opening the heart to live in present time with the emotions, healing the effects of trauma to free the body from the past, grounding into the earth to enliven the body, and connecting to nature to learn about the physical world. Opening the body to the movement of Kundalini is the eventual goal of such disciplines.

Essences - In spiritual work, the term essence refers to the true self—subtle energetic flows within the bodymind that are often isolated from connection to the world by the defenses and the ego identifications. When they are blocked and unexpressed, the individual has no connection to spiritual life. When these self structures are opened, spiritual transformation proceeds at a faster rate. Essence also refers to energy bands that surround holy and sacred places and resonate with the bodymind of those individuals who are able to open to what is present in those spaces. Compassion, love, will, strength, joy, peace, and value have been named as essential energies. Schools of spiritual development often focus on the development of specific essential states as a way to enhance direct, personal spiritual knowledge and connection. An individua's personal essence is a very formless aspect of the self in comparison with a role or a defensive structure.

Etheric energy - Etheric energy is the general term for the energy field structure that surrounds and penetrates living forms. It is called a subtle energy because of its relatively fine structure and the difficulty of making clear precise measurements of its movements. These fields can be detected by individuals with clairvoyant abilities and contain information about the health of the body and the thought structure of the individual. Many programs of psychospiritual development involve developing the ability to perceive these energies so the energy fields around the body (the aura) and the related anatomy of those fields (including the chakras) can be healed and strengthened.

Kundalini - The Kundalini is a natural (planetary) force associated with the creative process in physical forms. It exists as a potential energetic flow in all physical bodies.

In humans, the movement of this energy up the spine and throughout the body can bring change, purification, and an awareness of the transcendental. It is one of the most powerful exercises in blending and cannot be done without instruction, supervision, and prepration. The integration of Kundalini energy into the body has been a part of many schools of spiritual development, although there are wide differences in how the process is understood and approached. The original knowledge base for this experience comes from Tantric Yoga and the sacred writings of the Hindus.

Mediumship - Mediumship involves using the bodymind as a vehicle for the movement of extrapersonal energies (bands of energy not originating within the medium's own personal bodymind). It can involve the channeling of other non physical forms of consciousness (beings of all types and levels), running subtle bands of energy for healing or for the transmission of knowledge, speeding up the vibratory rate of the body to do psychic readings, or impacting the physical world (as in telekinesis and healing). There are many forms of mediumship, some acquired only genetically, some learned. Almost anyone can "channel" dissociated parts of him- or herselfs with instruction. Moving significant levels of extrapersonal energy requires both inborn talent and extensive training. It has been suggested that many powerful historical figures and spiritual teachers were probably transmediums, such as Christ, Hitler, Genghis Khan, Gurdjieff, Muktananda, and Meister Eckhart. Mediums often serve as bridges between the etheric (spiritual) and physical worlds because of their abilities to perceive life and movement in both worlds. Because their abilities involve the movement of extrapersonal energy, they can impact the world strongly and facilitate great good or great harm.

Possession - Possession also refers to states in which the individual's bodymind is being utilized as a vehicle for extrapersonal energies, including being used by others as an object. There are many levels of possession, ranging from removing choice from someone's potential expression, brainwashing a person to believe or behave a certain way, living tthrough an individual, allowing the body to serve as a vehicle for another's voice or energy, through the more spectacular forms of entity possession (as portrayed in the movie *The Exorcist*). Possession is always by agreement, although the agreement might be an unconscious choice. As described in the text, possession represents the absence of choiceful self-movements. Children, vulnerable adults, and mediums are most susceptible to possession, the former two because they do not have the ability or consciousness to say no and claim their own choice, the latter because they are often born with the genetic capability to allow other energies to coexist with the self system. Mediumship can be thought of as a temporary and choiceful possession. Because traumas (and other harmful experiences like substance abuse) can damage the development of the self, they can also make an individual more susceptible to possession.

Psychic - Psychic perception involves the development of a set of sensory organs beyond our usual five physical senses. It refers to the ability to perceive movement in the non physical world, including sensing the subtle energy fields around bodies, feeling subtle movements within the bodymind (as in intuition), sensing the non physical aspects of interactions between individuals (thoughts, feelings, or intentions), and sensing movement and forms in the non physical world (non physical beings, thought forms, or energetic processes). Many individuals have special skills in these areas, and many of these abilities can be learned in classes. Psychic development and spiritual development are not the same pursuit, but psychic skills are often developed as a part of psychospiritual growth since such work involves becoming more conscious of a universe that is vast, subtle, energetic, formless, and full of life.

Witness - The witness function (also called the observing self) is a mode of knowing about one's self structures and the world. The witness is the process of bringing awareness to thinking patterns, feeling states, and everyday functioning. The development of this experience represents the most important aspect of psychospiritual work since the bringing of consciousness to the self experience is the first prerequisite for change. The witness is a participatory and choiceful act of connection with one's external and internal worlds.

Notes

Preface: The Territory

1. Change can refer to either the enhancement or the reduction of an individual's abilities and connection. I am using the word *change* here in a particular way. I mean it to refer to the process of **transformation**—that is, changes in the individual that move toward the goal of development and the expansion of capacities.

2. I came in contact with the Teacher's work in 1984. Since that time, I have been an active participant in the process described here. In addition to the personal growth work, I have applied the principles to my work as a therapist. In the Teacher's work, there seemed to be three important factors that contributed to changes in students: one was the concepts taught and the expansion of awareness that came from seeing the universe in a different way; another was the strengthening of the abilities of the person to work with what was named in his or her own structures. The material in this book concerns itself with these two areas. A third factor was a dimension of energetic work and immediate contact with the Teacher's energy and level of consciousness. There were challenges in all three of these areas that provided both stimulation and the need to personally stretch to make deeper connections. From 1984 through 1989, the primary focus of the work was on personal development. In 1989 it switched to direct work with the Kundalini process and other forms of energetic work. Although most of the principles discussed in this essay were taught

to me in a setting in which the material was channeled, this is not a book of just channeled material. I have taken the general principles taught to me and applied them to the healing process, and I have only included the parts I have tested and worked with as a therapist and know to be powerful tools in change. The interpretation and application of these teachings are my own, and I have used material from psychology and other spiritual traditions to elaborate on the ideas.

Chapter 1: Change and the Experience of Space

1. In this essay, I am using the term *lie* to refer to an old form that was once a truth for the person, but no longer is functional. Lies are a major part of the defensive structure of many people. For example, if a person has a history of deprivation, he/she might have concluded that "I do not deserve love." At one time, this statement might have come from the energy of the parent, or have been concluded by the child on the basis of actual experience, but it is now a lie. It has no truth in the present, but is still operating as a belief in the psyche. It once was an answer, but now is a lie.

2. Throughout these chapters, I am using the word *structure* to refer to the organized patterns of perception and response that allow us to connect to the world. The terms *structures, psychophysical structures, ego structures, and bodymind structures,* all refer to the same basic idea— that the self experience is made up of the conscious recognition of these patterns of perception and response. Bringing more of these patterns into consciousness expands the self experience and makes it possible to alter them. A structure represents energy that is bound and contained, but also allows the movement of energy in such a way that connection is possible. In personal development, the focus is on the development of internal

structures that will facilitate our connection to the physical world and to other people. We seek healthy relationships and mastery of skills. In spiritual development, the internal structures required to connect to the etheric world require a different use of the mind and body. The perceptual side has to be developed to be able to sense and feel more subtle energetic movements, and the response side has to be developed to express the knowledge gained or triggered by the perceptions. To achieve this requires making very large shifts in how we perceive the world, think (believe), feel (act emotionally), and behave (connect). I have referred to those changes as structural shifts in the self experience.

3. This is a very general description of some of the ideas in Object Relations Theory. See Masterson, 1991.

Chapter 2 - Formlessness

1. *Locus of control* refers to the sets of stimuli that an individual attributes to controlling the choices he or she makes. If you have an external locus of control, you might perceive things as happening to you and your reactions based on things that impinge on you. Your focus is primarily on the outside world. An internal locus of control would mean that you make your choices based on your own perceptions, desires, and beliefs. As an individual's locus of control moves from external to internal, more of his or her internal depth process comes to the forefront and is a factor in his or her life choices.

2. There are a number of excellent papers in the transpersonal psychology literature that demonstrate the ability of meditation practices to work therapeutically. See Miller, 1993.

Chapter 3: The Formula for Change

    1. This model of the change process was first pro-
posed to students somewhere around 1978. I have seen
forms of it in the psychological literature in grief therapy
(Worden, 1982), in stress management (Flach, 1988), and
more recently, in the EMDR model (Shapiro, 1995).

    2. Most therapists will have interesting stories about
the reactions of people to having things named—from
having people feel deeply touched, to falling instantly
asleep, to going into shock, to exhibiting strong emotional
outbursts. You can feel suddenly "bonked" with a truth
or deeply understood by the other person. The most
general outcome is some alteration of the state of consciousness as the individual is consciously or unconsciously choosing to move toward or away from the
name. The game or structure is literally shattered by the
naming process and can, in some instances, shatter all
over everyone. This makes it better or worse depending
on the next choices made. Attack (by the mobilization
of defenses) is a very common reaction to naming behaviors that are abusive and prefer to remain unconscious or in denial. Therapist's skills are repeatedly challenged when they confront abusive or evil behaviors.

    3. There have been a number of popular therapies
that have been misinterpreted as the "naming of games"
(e.g. Transactional Analysis), and many therapists and
clients are aware of the abuse potential of having someone else name your games in an accusatory or judgmental way. You can also have things named out of your
timing or with little apparent regard for you as an individual. Similar considerations hold for psychic readings
in which unconscious material is brought to the surface
with little regard for the individual's preparedness for
the information or his or her ability to "move toward"
what was named (e.g., naming sexual abuse or childhood
traumas).

    4. Full use of the naming process is more appropri-

ate for students who have had therapy experience and are committed to deeper process work. It is not for everyone since it is so easily abused and requires an ability on the part of the student to regulate the timing of the process—to ask questions, to be able to say "stop," or "I need help," or "I'm feeling stuck." The foundation of the effectiveness of this experience is the ability to move toward whatever is named and allow the changes to occur that come from bringing deeper defensive structures into consciousness. This amounts to being challenged and held accountable for one's behavior (and energy) and its impact on others. Working with a teacher and having a support group are important parts of the experience. It also requires a good ability to work with the energies of formlessness.

5. See Figure 8.

6. The psychologist's name was Arthur M. Anton, Ph.D. of Santa Clara, California. He shared this statement with us and gave permission to share it with others. He uses it in the treatment of chronic pain problems.

7. Each of the core belief systems of an individual is made up of a number of different subsystems—a set of cognitions and sentences about the self (the actual belief that is operating); psychic pictures, images and memories accoaiated with the formation of the belief; the emotions associated with the formation, and the initial responses one made to the experiences. These structures form the "biochemical envelope" of the belief. All of the different parts will emerge and have to be worked with when the disorganization begins. The processing of trauma in the bodymind is an example of this process "in extremis." It takes both great courage and consciousness to change these formations.

Chapter 4 - Light and Darkness

1. One might summarize schools of recovery, personal growth, and spiritual development in general as consisting of three major emphases: (1) finding the support and strength to cease destructive and/or limiting behaviors; (2) Strengthening the healthy parts of the self, and (3) Bringing the unhealthy or dark parts into consciousness and working with them, using the strengthened healthy parts. The literature of spiritual development is filled with literally hundreds of ways to do the first two stages. Healthy parts of the self become strengthened by acknowledging the body and its needs (through diet, exercise, bodywork, movement, etc.); by forming healthy belief systems and expanding our knowledge of spiritual development in other cultures and esoteric systems; and by increasing the range of our capacities to touch both physical and spiritual realities more deeply (e.g., altered state work or psychic development). Almost all schools of spiritual development have training in this aspect of psychospiritual work. There is, however, a line crossed when the growth process includes the integration of the dark side. The support requirements go way up as do the abilities required of the individuals involved.

2. Two examples of this are the "tough love" approaches to adolescent acting out and attempts by some European countries to deal with the drug problem (notably the Netherlands). They both attempt to (1) contact the problem (the people involved) rather than let it go on underground, and (2) bring "healthy" resources to bear, namely to be open to looking at how the system has to change in order to solve the problem. These approaches work so long as the healthy side of the family or the culture stays stronger than the dark side. The healthy side must have a good support system, that is, be operating in an interdependent framework in which resources can be tapped when needed.

3. The formulation here is similar to a story of creation that involves the fall of Lucifer. As it is told, Lucifer was a powerful angel and once part of the Godhead. His fall (his separation from God) and subsequent refusal to reconnect and lose his individual powers led to the forces of evil in the world. This folklore legend contains the essence of the idea of evil—that it is the forces of destruction **isolated and disconnected** from the creative process as a whole (the Godhead) and is perpetuated by the unwillingness to connect back and be changed by that connection. In one version of the legend, God created the world, sent the creations out with choice, and made the reconnection optional. It is Lucifer's choice to stay separate. It is that choice that keeps him evil.

4. One could say that the parents are the first "soul" to the body of the child. As maturity increases, these teachings are eventually challenged and usually replaced by the goals and purposes that emerge from within.

5. I am appreciative for the help of Dr. Stephen Bolles for his assistance in forming the scar tissue analogy.

6. These structures are only four of many structural configurations that make up the structure of the psyche. Buddhist psychology has described many more—see for example the list in the appendix of Varela, et.al. The four I have described are the ones often seen in emotional healing work.

7. This phenomenon is known to those who work with the Victim-Perpetrator-Rescuer triangle. One role may be identified with as more familiar, but in the healing process, all three roles will surface and be seen as part of the behaviors of the individual. Thus the victim position always also includes perpetration and rescuing.

8. This is often the most difficult part of becoming more sensitive to the world as part of psychospiritual work. What to do and how to act in the face of world pain and evil. To embrace bodily experience and feel emotions more deeply requires that defenses be relin-

quished. This experience is often painful for people when the perceptions open before they knows how to erect boundaries against negativity or act to protect themselves.

Chapter 5: Creative Disorganization

1. This concept of the "spiritual emergency" was developed by Christina and Stan Grof in their work with individuals in transpersonal crisis. The spiritual emergency is a state of temporary disruption that occurs in the personality structure or life style as part of an awakening of the person's spiritual life. These might be experiences of psychic opening, mystical experiences, near-death experiences, Kundalini awakening, or even the shifts in consciousness that occur in the mid life crisis. They often are accompanied by intense altered-state experiences and result in profound changes in belief systems and life styles. The Grofs cofounded the Spiritual Emergency Network to provide support and education for individuals experiencing these states.

2. A good place to begin with these clinical procedures is with material by Winnecott (1974) and Hedges (1994). See also Eigen (1986). Certain agonizing and terrifying experiences that occur very early in childhood are not remembered because they were never consciously experienced by the developing infant, or were not organized verbally, or were captured as a part of a different, non rational bodymind state. Their presence is often indicated by the addictive/compulsive behavior of the adult that both seeks and fears situations in which these feelings are experienced. In these cases, the disorganization of the defenses and the integration of those experiences has to be done in a present-time holding environment with present-time relationships for healing to occur. The therapeutic work involves integrating very formless bodymind states in which there are few memories or images to help define the experience.

Chapter 6: Voids, Chaos, and Formlessness

1. There are many sources of "foreign energies" in the bodymind. They come from all the people who have defined the child, the school systems that influence and control the expressions, and the atmospheres and energies of the family and social environment that surround the child. When these infusions of energy and "answers" are not able to be questioned, possession results. Individuals who have had possession as a part of their childhood experience will often seek it as adults—"Tell me what to do and who I am."

2. Chaos as a self experience has been commented on by a number of current writers in psychotherapy and is known as the "psychotic core" experience (Eigen, 1993). It goes without saying that therapeutic approaches to these problems require great sensitivity and skill. It does not help to expose the voids without the ability to form the question to negotiate the formless experience.

3. The experience of The Void referred to in many spiritual texts and as part of the Dark Night of the Soul experience is such an example of a higher order of complexity. The Void is not an empty space, but an Ocean of Life of such complexity and fluidity that it is difficult to maintain and sustain a conscious connection. Experiences like the Dark Night of the Soul represent a shift in the individual's consciousness and in previous levels of psychic structure so that connection is possible to still more complex orders. Meanwhile, the original connection is lost.

Chapter 7: Reorganization

1. See the work of L. Hedges (1994) for how to work with clients for whom the "organizing process" has not

developed. His work teaches therapists to address these early emotional developmental deficits in a sensitive and knowledgeable way.

2. I am regarding the question as the minimum structure necessary for the further development of forms of healthy behaviors. At the cognitive level, specific sentences could be used as interweaves as they are in healing/blending work; structured affirmations provide healthy information; concepts and stories provide knowledge and direction; myths can contain enough formlessness that they can be healing for many different kinds of voids. Similar considerations apply for bodywork. The basic "question" would be bodily awareness of sensations and self-movements. Further help with new answers would involve learning specific exercises and emotional movements, or facilitating spontaneous movements in the body. More formless systems of bodywork in which deep self movements are encouraged (such as authentic movement or process-oriented bodywork) would allow many new answers to emerge.

Chapter 8: Healing and Blending

1. These exercises are beyond the scope of this text. Many of the processes the Teacher has taught involve the blending of several different energetic movements and structures, including grounding, integrating the chakras, facilitating the movement of Kundalini, and working with nature forms. They involve the development and maintenance of many different energy movements and extend the blending process beyond touching the dark side.

2. In this text, I have only described the healing process in very general terms. I am familiar with a number of systems that directly involve blending as part of the

healing process: (1) Vipassana meditation in which awareness is blended with all contents of mind that arise during practice. This gentle form of blending brings choice into the contents of consciousness through naming and the refocusing of awareness; (2) EMDR—Eye Movement Desensitization and Reprocessing (Shapiro, 1995)—a therapeutic process in which trauma structures are opened through eye movements and other rhythmic patterns. The healing process involves facilitating the emergence of "adaptive information processing" and using cognitive interweaves to form the basis of the linkage between the wound and the healthy sides of the individual; (3) the "Somatic Re-experiencing" shock and trauma work of Dr. Peter Levine (Levine, 1990), in which the orienting response and motor movements are restored to the frozen traumatized body; (4) the "rescripting" processes used in Transactional Analysis and in neurofeedback work (Budzynsky, 1993); (5) supportive, empathic psychotherapy. All of these methodologies have devised ways to bring the wound structures into consciousness and blend these ego states with new information inputs to change the functioning of the self system.

Chapter 9: Living in the Question

1. See Almaas, 1986; Welwood, 1977; Epstein, 1988; and Loy, 1992 for discussions of the process by which space is brought into the self experience.

Selected Bibliography

Almaas, A. H. *The Void*, Berkeley: Diamond Books, Almaas Publications, 1986.

Assagioli, Roberto. *Psychosynthesis*. New York: Viking Press, 1965.

Bragdon, Emma. *The Call of Spiritual Emergency*. New York: Harper & Row, 1990.

Bridges, William. *Transitions*. New York: AddisonWesley, 1980.

Budzynski, Thomas. *Clinical Guide to Light/Sound*. Seattle: Synetic Systems, Inc. 1993.

Eigen, Michael. *The Psychotic Core*. New Jersey: Jason Aronson, 1993.

Epstein, Mark. "The Deconstruction of the Self: Ego and 'Egolessness' in Buddhist Insight Meditation." *J. Transpersonal Psychology*, 20(1), 61-69,1988.

Flach, Frederic. *Resilience*. New York: Fawcett Columbine, 1988.

Gleick, James. *Chaos: Making a New Science*. New York: Penguin Books, 1987.

Grof, Stanislav and Christina Grof (ed.). *Spiritual Emergency: When Personal Transformation Becomes a Crisis*. Los Angeles: Jeremy P. Tarcher, 1989.

Growe, David. *Restructuring Memories*. Minneapolis: Workshop material, 1985.

Hager, Drevis. "Chaos and Growth." *Psychotherapy*, 29(3), 378-384, 1992.

Hedges, Lawrence. *Working the Organizing Experience: Transforming Psychotic, Schizoid, & Autistic States*. New Jersey: Jason Aronson, 1994.

Houston, Jean. *Creating Miracles.* Minneapolis: Work-
    shop material, 1994.

Jantsch, Erich. *The Self-Organizing Universe.* New York:
    Pergamon Press, 1980.

Keleman, Stanley. *Somatic Reality.* Berkeley: Center
    Press, 1979.

Kris, E. "On Preconscious Mental Processes." *Psycho-
    analytic Quarterly,* 19, 540-560, 1950.

Levine, Peter. "The Body as Healer: A Revisioning of
    Trauma and Anxiety." *Somatics,* 8(1), 18-27, 1990.

Loy, David. "Avoiding the Void: The Lack of Self in
    Psychotherapy and Buddhism." *J. Transpersonal
    Psychology,* 24(2), 151-179, 1992.

Masterson, James. *Comparing Psychoanalytic
    Psychotherapies: Developmental; Self and Object Relations;
    Self Psychology; Short Term Dynamic.* New York: Bruner/
    Mazel, 1991.

Miller, John. "The Unveiling of Traumatic Memories and
    Emotions through Mindfulness and Concentration
    Meditation." *J. Transpersonal Psychology,* 28(2), 169-180,
    1993.

Mindell, Arnold. *Rivers Way.* New York: Routledge &
    Kegan, 1985.

Muller-Schwefe, Rudolf. "Pulsation." *Energy and
    Character,* 22(2), 32-50, 1994.

Prigogine, Ilya. *Order Out of Chaos: Man's New Dialogue
    with Nature.* New York: Bantam Books, 1994.

Shapiro, Francine. *Eye Movement Desensitization and
    Reprocessing: Basic Principles, Protocols and Procedures.*
    New York: Guilford Publications, 1995.

St. John of the Cross. "The Dark Night," *John of the Cross:
    Selected Writings.* New York: Paulist Press, 1979.

Tweedie, Irina. *The Chasm of Fire.* England: Element
    Books, 1979.

Underhill, Evelyn. *Practical Mysticism.* Columbus: Ariel
    Press, 1942.

Varela, Francisco, Evan Thompson and Eleanor Rosch.
    The Embodied Mind. Cambridge: The MIT Press, 1991.

Welwood, John. "On Psychological Space." *J. Transpersonal Psychology*, 9(2), 97-118, 1977.

Winnecott, D.W. "Fear of Breakdown.""*Int. Rev. Psycho-Anal.* 1, 103-107, 1974.

Worden, J. William. *Grief Counseling and Grief Therapy.* New York: Springer Publishing, 1982.

Zweig, Connie and Jeremiah Abrams. (ed.). *Meeting the Shadow.* Los Angeles: Jeremy P. Tarcher, 1991.

Index

About the Author

Michael J. Maley, Ph.D. graduated from the Massachusetts Institute of Technology in 1961 and from the University of Minnesota Graduate School in Psychology in 1967. He holds a bachelor's degree from the College of Traditional Chinese Medicine (United Kingdom), is a member of the teaching faculty of the International Institute for Bioenergetic Analysis, and was a regional coordinator for the Spiritual Emergence Network from 1987 through 1994. He is a practicing clinical psychologist in Minneapolis, Minnesota, specializing in the treatment of trauma and mood disorders. His clinical work is a blend of several alternative and traditional therapeutic methods, including Bioenergetic Analysis, EMDR, and subtle energy work. He also teaches seminars internationally on somatic psychotherapy, personal transformation, and healing.

Order Form

Name _____

Address_____

City_____State_____

Country_____Postal Code_____

Phone (____)_____ ☐ day ☐ evening

<u># of copies</u>   @   <u>price</u>   +   <u>shipping**</u>   =   <u>total charges</u>

_____   x **$13.95**   +   _____   =   _____

Send this order form & your check or money order to:

Bodysmart Publications
P.O. Box 1184
Minnetonka, MN 55345-0184

Shipping & Handling Charges: Enclose **$3.00 for the first book ordered, plus **$ .50** for each additional book shipped to the same address in the same order.

Orders from Canada and other countries: Payment in US currency only. Foreign orders are shipped surface.

Allow 3-4 weeks for delivery.

For orders of 10 or more books, the cost is $11.95 per book. Shipping charges are the same.

Order Form

Name _____

Address _____

City _____ **State** _____

Country _____ **Postal Code** _____

Phone (___ **)** _____ ☐ **day** ☐ **evening**

# of copies	@ price	+	shipping**	=	total charges
_____	x **$13.95** +		_____	=	_____

Send this order form & your check or money order to:

Bodysmart Publications
P.O. Box 1184
Minnetonka, MN 55345-0184

Shipping & Handling Charges : Enclose **$3.00 for the first book ordered, plus **$ .50** for each additional book shipped to the same address in the same order.

Orders from Canada and other countries : Payment in US currency only. Foreign orders are shipped surface.

Allow 3-4 weeks for delivery.

For orders of 10 or more books, the cost is $11.95 per book. Shipping charges are the same.